DRIVE, RIDE, REPEAT

The Mostly-True Account of a Cross-Country Car and Bicycle Adventure

By Al Macy
http://AlMacyStuff.com

Also by Al Macy:

Becoming a Great Sight-Reader—or Not! Learn from my Quest for Piano Sight-Reading Nirvana

TABLE OF CONTENTS

Acknowledgments...5
Prologue...7
Chapter One
Meet Al (That's Me)...10
Chapter Two
Shakedown Cruise...13
Chapter Three
Meet the Napinator...14
Chapter Four
Meet Lena...15
Chapter Five
Al Gets His Checkboxes Checked......................................18
Chapter Six
Meet Britta the Animal...20
Chapter Seven
Who's a Tightwad?..22
Chapter Eight
Snow Camping..25
Chapter Nine
Zero Dark Hundred...28
Chapter Ten
Meet Our Bikes...33
Chapter Eleven
Al Gets a Tattoo..36
Chapter Twelve
Bad News Brain Tumor...40
Chapter Thirteen
A Big Win in Vegas!...43
Chapter Fourteen
Al Crashes...45
Chapter Fifteen
Crashes—Cycling's Dark Side...47

Chapter Sixteen
War Driving...50
Chapter Seventeen
Lena Breaks a National Monument.....................................52
Chapter Eighteen
Meet My Mom...56
Chapter Nineteen
Picking Up Hitchhikers...59
Chapter Twenty
Camping is Dead..63
Chapter Twenty-One
Shorts in the Snow..66
Chapter Twenty-Two
More Flats...70
Chapter Twenty-Three
Kidnapped!..72
Chapter Twenty-Four
Supergluing the Car...75
Chapter Twenty-Five
Killer Tornado..77
Chapter Twenty-Six
Meet Jenny..79
Chapter Twenty-Seven
Jenny Actually Graduates..81
Chapter Twenty-Eight
Pack It Up...85
Chapter Twenty-Nine
And Move It Out..87
Chapter Thirty
Everything Burned..89
Chapter Thirty-One
An Echo Echo...92
Chapter Thirty-Two
A Major Mishap—Finally!..95
Chapter Thirty-Three
Pepsi Cooking...98
Chapter Thirty-Four
Secret Dakota Child Labor...100
Chapter Thirty-Five
Al Works a Silver Mine...103
Chapter Thirty-Six
Explosive Show..107

Chapter Thirty-Seven
More Wacky Inventions..110
Chapter Thirty-Eight
Al's Lycra Causes a Stampede.......................................115
Chapter Thirty-Nine
Lena Holds Back a Glacier...118
Chapter Forty
Visit From a Monster...121
Chapter Forty-One
The Land of Big Bowling Balls.....................................123
Chapter Forty-Two
Old Somewhat Faithful..126
Chapter Forty-Three
Low Gravity...129
Chapter Forty-Four
Good Luck is Bad Luck...132
Chapter Forty-Five
Al's Bicycling Tips...134
Chapter Forty-Six
Back to the Snow..140
Chapter Forty-Seven
Puking in a Thunderstorm..142
Chapter Forty-Eight
Home Sweet (and Foggy) Home....................................144
Epilogue..146
Would You Do Me a Favor?..148
About the Author..149

ACKNOWLEDGMENTS

Many thanks to my wonderful proofreader (and wife) Lena, who despite being a born-and-raised Swede, speaks English better than most Americans. Plus, she puts up with me.

Steve Lord, a good childhood friend who you'll meet at several places in this book, was an insightful and thorough editor. Many thanks to him for fine-tuning my recollections and pointing out problems that needed correcting.

Thanks also to Janine, my sisters (Carol, Linda, and Gail), KCowan, Lara, Marie, Bob, Andy, Rosie, REWahoo, Dudelsak, Sengsational, Coogie, and all the others I roped into providing free editing.

PROLOGUE

Welcome to the journal of our car/bike/camp trip from California to St. Louis and back.

Now, hold on, I know what you're saying: "Journal? Oh boy, here it comes: 'Today we went here, and then we turned left, and we drove to that town, and we had crackers and tomato soup, and I got diarrhea, and then we visited Aunt Joan.'"

No, it's not going to be like that at all, except for maybe the diarrhea part. I promise that if it starts sounding like one of your brother-in-law's boring slide shows, I will stop this book, and we'll turn around and go home. I mean it.

My wife (Lena) and I ride our bikes a lot, so when we travel, we bring our bikes and do day rides. This way, we avoid the hardships of real bicycle touring, yet can still feel snobbishly superior to the other tourists.

We have, of course, planned the trip in minute detail. I have written down this plan, and here it is:

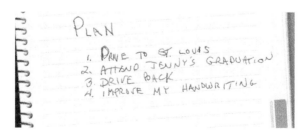

7

The plan also includes numerous charts and maps. Well, one map:

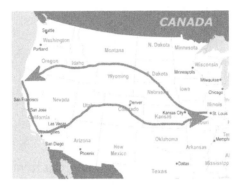

In case you find our adventures too stimulating, and need a break, I have interspersed the journal chapters with thought-provoking life tips, stories from my past, and descriptions of my wacky inventions. You'll read about puking in a thunderstorm, and how Morfar's buddy swallowed a trumpet. You'll hear poignant anecdotes about what happened when doctors discovered a golf-ball-sized tumor in my wife's brain and how everything we owned burned. Here's an example of the kind of stories you'll read:

A few years ago, I needed advice on setting up payroll for my small company, and drove down to my accountant's office to speak with his assistant. It was an informal operation—the kind with overstuffed chairs, worn rugs, and an office dog. A few weeks after this meeting, I called and said "Hi, I have some questions about the payroll system, could I please speak to Sadie?" Unfortunately, I hadn't really paid attention to the names, and it turned out that "Sadie" was the name of the office dog. So now, whenever I go there, I expect them to whistle for Sadie, in case I want to ask her about stock options or retirement plans.

So, those are the kinds of stories you have to look forward to if the journal gets too exciting. Someone suggested that I make them "sidebars," but since I don't know what a sidebar is, I'll just put them in their own chapters.

Concerning photos, apparently having hundreds of pictures in a book is some kind of literary faux pas (well, excuse me!), so I've limited myself to one or two photos per chapter. I cried a little when I stripped out the excess pictures, because I really like photos (especially my own), but I still have binders full of photos (and some videos) on the web. So for the full brother-in-law slide show experience, follow the links on my author web site, AlMacyStuff.com.

CHAPTER ONE
MEET AL (THAT'S ME)

My great-grandfather was born in a small village … Ha ha, don't you hate it when you read a biography, and it starts several generations back? So I'll skip all that and give it to you in a nutshell: I'm a character and a cheapskate who married a frugal wife. We were able to squirrel away our money so that we could retire early and do interesting things. While working, I was a neuroscientist (with a real PhD), a computer game programmer, a jazz musician, a chef, a CEO, a clam digger, and a technical writer.

By the way, for these childhood memories, I'll invoke a quotation from Mark Twain: "When I was younger I could remember anything, whether it happened or not; but I am getting old, and soon I shall remember only the latter."

I do remember that when in school, I was the class clown. For example, here's a joke that I played on my best friend Steve—it's something I'd never do today.

We were at the ocean on the south shore of Long Island. I decided to make him think I'd drowned. Nice friend, right? Somehow I was able to swim far enough underwater that I could come up undetected down the beach a bit. I even got up onto the shore behind Steve without him noticing. We were on a deserted section of ocean, and according to Steve, one minute I was there, and the next minute, gone. He grew more and more panicky, and ran back and forth trying to see me, yelling my name. When I came up behind him, laughing, he was relieved but angry. Terrible joke, huh? He still mentions it when we see each other.

That kind of humor gets socialized out of you. For example, a few years ago my older sisters were visiting me in Oakland, CA, and they were out walking on a deserted road. I was running, and I snuck up behind them and made a roaring noise like a bear. They both jumped off the ground. One farted and clutched her heart and the other wet her pants. So, although that sense of humor is inside me, I've had to learn to control it before I kill someone.

Perhaps the bear noise prank was some kind of unconscious payback for something that happened when I was six. My older sister was babysitting me while my parents were having a party. I'd probably been watching some crime show, and I wanted to know if I could get loose if I were tied up. So Sis tied me up, and even gagged me, as per my instructions, with a red bandanna. She then went down to the party and forgot all about me. I spent hours trying to get loose, and managed to fall between the bed and a table, with my sweaty, tear-streaked face down among the dust bunnies. My sister says that when she finally remembered, she raced up to free me, and as soon as she got my hands untied, I started hitting her.

The funny thing about that is that although this still haunts my sister to this day (she apologizes every time she sees me), I have absolutely no memory of it—the description above is from what she's recounted.

In this next picture, taken in 1964, I'm the one holding the milk, and the blonde on the left is the one still holding the emotional scars from that episode.

One more story (and it's bike related) to show you what I'm like: When I was 13, I had a steering wheel on my bicycle. I somehow bolted an old steering wheel from a junkyard onto the bike's stem. It actually worked quite well (the bike had coaster brakes), and it let me use my favorite joke: "What's the most unreliable part on a vehicle? It's the nut that holds the steering wheel."

So, enough about me. Let's get to the trip, and I promise not to play any tricks on you.

CHAPTER TWO
SHAKEDOWN CRUISE

April 21, 2009—Gold Bluffs Beach, CA: To check that we had everything we'd need, and especially to check out the air mattress that I'd gotten for $4 at a garage sale, we went on a quick one-night camping shakedown trip.

Camping isn't much fun if you aren't comfortable sleeping. If you're counting the minutes until dawn and wishing you were on a nice, soft bed of nails, you're not going to be a … well, a happy camper. So a good mattress is job one.

The garage-sale mattress was in like-new condition. As comfortable as our mattress at home, it fit in the tent like a cork in a wine bottle. The pump inflated and deflated it in about one minute using four rechargeable AA cells (in D cell adapters).

At 1 AM, something was up, and I started dreaming I was on a waterbed. By 3:30 AM the mattress had deflated completely, without any assistance from the batteries, and we were *on the hard ground*. This is the ground that has gotten significantly harder since turning 50 (I was 56 when we made this trip). Since the mattress fit the tent so snugly, we had to get outside to blow it up again, and it stayed inflated until morning. When I got home, I tracked down the leak and repaired it with PVC cement and duct tape. This sounds kludgey, but it is the officially sanctioned procedure.

But we had a good time in general, and a great breakfast of eggs, bacon, and home-baked bread. All systems were go for our trip.

CHAPTER THREE
MEET THE NAPINATOR

April 16, 2009—Home: We didn't want this trip to interfere with our favorite hobby, napping, so it was time for one of Al's wacky inventions: The Napinator.

The main reason I can't sleep in trains, planes, or automobiles is that my head falls to one side, and I wake up. Those little blowup neck pillows have never worked for me; I need something made out of scrap lumber. The Napinator is just the ticket, and will keep our respective heads from rolling from side to side while sleeping in the car. Slip out the normal headrest, slip in this torture-device, add a soft pillow, and it's nap time.

CHAPTER FOUR
MEET LENA

Time for some background on my wife. Lena is not a "character." If you were to say to her friends, "Boy, that Lena sure is a character!" They would squint, look at you as if you had tiny monkeys coming out of your nose, and say, "Who, Lena Macy?" I tested this, and that is precisely what all her friends said, except one who said: "Are those tiny monkeys coming out of your nose?"

Lena is a level-headed, born-and-raised Swede. She was born above the Arctic Circle, in JokkMokk, which is pronounced "Yuck-Muck." I had her pronounce it carefully for me, because I figured you wouldn't believe me. Her personality complements my wacky inherited traits, just as her steady chemical engineer income was the perfect counterpoint to my up and down revenue stream.

This is not to say that Lena doesn't enjoy life. She's a lot better at that than I am, actually, although you wouldn't know it by looking at her facial expressions. When she's at rest, she may be happy on the inside, but if you look at her, you'll want to put her on suicide watch. She got that from her family. Here's a 1999 photo of Jenny, Lena's Mom, Lena, and Lena's dad having a rollicking good time.

Apparently Lena's grandfather was, in contrast, a character, and there are many stories to back that up. In Swedish, the term for a grandparent is based on precise lineage. For example, "morfar" (pronounced "moor - far") translates to "mother father" and means your mother's father. "Farfar" would be the father of your father. "Morfarsmor" would be your mother's father's mother. Get it?

It's not a bad system, and is shorter than saying, for example, "My great-grandfather on my mother's side, and her grandfather's side." Luckily, nobody cares about ancestry in the USA, so we don't have to sweat those kinds of details.

Anyway, Lena's morfar Alex (pronounced "Ah-lex") was a colorful character. During World War I, when he was in the King's Technical College in Stockholm, his dorm room had a bed with a big brass knob on it. There was a standing competition to see if anyone could open his jaw wide enough to put his mouth around the knob. No one had ever succeeded until Alex's red-haired buddy Sven, his jaw loosened by large quantities of alcohol, finally did it.

Unfortunately, it turned out that it's much harder to get your mouth off of a big brass knob than it is to get it on, and Sven was stuck. Nothing worked, and no amount of grease or prying helped. The knob wouldn't even slide around in his mouth. Luckily, they discovered that by lifting Sven up, and rotating his body counterclockwise around the post, they could unscrew the knob.

It was now 3 AM, and they set off for the hospital for a knob-ectomy. You'd think that having a big brass knob stuck in your mouth would make you rather subdued, but apparently that was not the case. The group was so rowdy and noisy, in fact, that they were written up for "förargelseväckande beteende" (disorderly conduct). The police report, which is now famous in Lena's family, included the phrase "Och den vildaste av alla bråkmakare var pojken som hade svalt en trumpet" which translates to "And the rowdiest troublemaker of all was the one who had swallowed a trumpet."

OK, enough background. From California, well below the Arctic Circle, we were ready to get our show on the road.

CHAPTER FIVE
AL GETS HIS CHECKBOXES CHECKED

April 30, 2009—Departure: I always forget how much work packing is. One month of stuff for two people, plus bikes and gear, had to be crammed into a Toyota Echo. We pretty much spent all of yesterday packing.

Packing is crucial. I didn't want to get to our first campsite and realize that we'd forgotten the tent poles, for example, especially since that actually happened on a childhood family camping trip. Right after my mom said "Well, I guess you could call us experienced campers now," we looked in the tent bag and came up empty. As a result, the "experienced campers" slept in a saggy umbrella tent tied to a tree branch.

Because of experiences like that, my life is ruled by checklists, man's best invention. I have checklists for fishing, surfing, biking, piano gigs, skiing, changing the oil, and just going to town (keys, wallet, cell phone, change). This trip required going through the bike ride checklist, the camping checklist, the long-trip checklist, and the leaving-the-house-for-a-trip checklist (water off, heat off, fridge closed).

[If you're not a checklist enthusiast, please skip the next paragraph.]

As a true checklist connoisseur, I know that there are three types of checklists with subtle but important differences: (1) to do lists, (2) shopping lists, and (3) true checklists. Want to remember to pay your bills every month? Use the to do list. Want to remember what to pick up at the store? Use the shopping list. Don't want to take a bike ride without your helmet? Use a true checklist before you leave. I've now automated my lists by getting checklist apps for my android device, and for those

18

three categories of lists, I use Remember the Milk (which is actually not good for remembering the milk), OI Shopping list, and List Master Pro, respectively.

There are lots of ways to abuse a checklist. One is to forget to use it. Another is to, for example, check off "Water Bottle," but only put the water bottle *near* but not *on* your bike. The third is to go through the list absent-mindedly, saying "Got it" when you don't got it.

There are some people who think that checklists are for sissies. They're the ones saying "Oh, Jeez, did I leave the oven on?"

In addition to going through the checklists, and in true tightwad fashion, I totaled up the cash in our pockets so that I could, upon our return, figure out exactly how much this trip cost.

Everything fit in our tiny, fuel-efficient 2002 Echo, and (trumpets sounding) off we went.

An uneventful eight hours, and two traffic jams later we arrived in the Bay Area. Most importantly, we discovered that the napinator works great. I'd patent it, but then I'd have to deal with the whiplash liability claims.

We arrived at the Moraga home of our good friends, Ted and Britta, and Britta cooked a fantastic dinner. Then we went to a rave.

Chapter Six
Meet Britta the Animal

May 1, 2009—Bay Area Visit

Day 2 at Ted and Britta's was the first bike ride day of the trip. This is the "ride" part of the "Drive, Ride, Repeat" title.

About my biking: I'm not very fast. I ride a lot, and I can do a century ride (a group 100-mile ride), but compared with most MAMILs (Middle Aged Men in Lycra) I'm a slow poke (and yes, I realize that at 56 I'm no longer middle-aged). For my last century, my average speed was 13.9 MPH, which means I came to the finish after the beer was gone. Lena is a stronger rider than I, and if she wanted to work at it, could really kick my butt.

Speaking of middle-aged. When I was 35, Lena and I were robbed at gunpoint. The guy jumped out of the bushes, stuck a huge gun at my belly, and said "Give me your f**king wallet!" I just handed it over, and didn't say "Actually, I don't have a f**king wallet, but I have a regular wallet. Will that do?"

For some reason, the experience was more interesting than scary, but the scary part was yet to come. The next day the local newspaper ran a story that started with "Last night a middle-aged couple ..." "Middle-aged! What? We're not ... oh, wait a second ..." That was a rude awakening, and if you've seen the movie *The Others*, it was like the scene where the kids are screaming, "We're *not* dead, we're *not* dead!" We were yelling "We're *not* middle-aged, we're *not* middle-aged!"

Back to the trip, Lena took the day off, and as soon as Britta got her coffee doping infusion, she and I headed off for a 30-mile ride to Skyline

Drive, on the ridge above Berkeley and Oakland. We had planned to ride up Mount Diablo (she rides up the mountain once a week, which I see as a sign of mental illness), but there was rain in the forecast so we settled for this ride instead.

Britta is an animal, and dropped me on all the hills. If you're not a cyclist, "drop" means that by the time I got to the top, she'd read two novels and taken a nap. My consolation was that her chain fell off her $3,000 bike. Twice.

Ted and Britta have a little dog named "Sophie." It's some kind of Lassie Apso, or Cocka Shitzel. I'll now draw on my vast scientific background to tell you something about dogs. Here is an actual brain of a dog:

The lightning bolt things are neuroses attempting to enter the dog's brain. Large dogs have a "dog brain barrier" (Canis cerebrum obice) which keeps the neuroses from entering the brain. That barrier is absent in small dogs.

Here is Sophie's main neurosis: she has a doggie door that she knows how to use, and can use without any physical assistance. However, when she wants to go out or in she won't use it until someone comes into the room and says "OK!" in a perky voice. She will pee in the house rather than go through the door without someone saying "OK!"

Her other neurosis is that she eats Britta's underwear. So, she has that in common with Ted.

CHAPTER SEVEN
WHO'S A TIGHTWAD?

I don't want to sound preachy here, so I'll just say that being tightwads has worked out well for us. We've never felt deprived. Being retired since our early fifties, and doing whatever we want each day, is priceless. Every day feels like the first day of summer vacation.

People fall into three groups. Those in the first group, the natural-born tightwads group, innately understand the advantages of being a frugalista. They seek out and appreciate tips for saving money. Those in the second group have an inner tightwad that may need awakening or encouragement. But people in the third group, the spenders group, don't understand why some people are thrifty. They usually feel like they deserve to buy the things they do. I'm not judging, this can work fine for them. However, there's something that people in this group need to do immediately: Skip to the next chapter.

Some people will say, "You need to have balance," meaning you have to evaluate the trade-offs between spending now and saving for later. Definitely true, but realize that until every day is your own, you can't appreciate how nice it is. If starting over, I'd probably aim to retire at age 45.

Some people say, "I'll keep my job. I don't love it, but I'd be way too bored if I weren't working. What would I do all day?" That's fine, but just realize that what they are really saying is, "I am not able to think of things to do, so I need to have someone else tell me how to spend my time."

Perhaps it's just me, but I rarely find myself bored. Each day I wake up with nothing to do, and by the end of the day, I've only gotten half of it done.

If you want to embrace your inner tightwad, here are some things that have worked for me.

- Research frugality. Check out the many web sites that have tips and tricks for saving money. Read the classic *Tightwad Gazette*, and other books on this topic.

- Make investing your hobby. Read all you can from books and the internet. It's not rocket science. You may find that you can take just as much pleasure from watching your savings balance grow as you can from spending money. There are simple solutions to how to invest (for example, Vanguard Target Retirement Funds); the only hard thing about investing is avoiding advice from people who don't have your best interests at heart.

- Concentrate on cutting down on recurring (for example, monthly) expenses, and think about how the savings would add up over a ten-year period.

- Help your kids financially only until they've finished college. You won't be doing them any favors by providing assistance after that.

- Choose your hobbies carefully. Investing, making things you can use or sell, or reading are good frugal hobbies. Collecting, aka buying things you don't need just so you can *have them*—not so much.

Here are some examples of how much you can save by reducing recurring expenses.

Haircuts: In 2000, When Jenny was 12, I got a book from the library entitled *Scissors and Comb Haircutting: A Cut-by-Cut Guide*, and told Jenny that I'd pay her to cut my hair. She learned quickly, and even the first haircut looked fine. When Jenny left for college, she passed the skill on to Lena. The average cost of a haircut in this country (in 2014) is $17, so since I bought that book I've saved over $2,800 in my monthly haircuts (or at least kept that money in the family). We could save lots more if Lena would let me near her hair with the clippers.

Electricity Usage: I have a friend who leaves his outdoor lights on 24/7. It costs him under a buck a day, but over 10 years he'd save $2,700 if he'd just flip the switch to off. By conserving electricity, you can drop down into lower rate tiers, saving a surprising amount of money.

Garage and Rummage Sales: You'll scoff at discounts of 20% or 50% once you get used to the 90% discounts common at garage sales. You may have to visit eight sales before you find something you need, but if you plan out a good route, you won't waste much gas, and you'll have fun. Craigslist purchases fall into this category as well.

Fix Things Yourself: When the dryer goes on strike, or the dishwasher decides to rinse the floor instead of the dishes, it's intimidating. You just want to hide behind something and call the repair person. But I've been surprised at how often a little online investigation (ApplianceAssistant.com, for example), will lead to a simple fix. Every one of our major appliances has had a breakdown that turned out to be fixable with a tweak or a small part ordered via the internet. You can save a lot here, and you may find that it's rewarding to get things working on your own. Your spouse will say things like "You're awesome!" or "Wouldn't it have been easier just to call someone?"

Everyone's different. Perhaps a frugal life followed by a long retirement isn't for you, but if you're like me, it's worth every penny saved.

CHAPTER EIGHT
SNOW CAMPING

May 2, 2009—Moraga to Sequoia: After a good night's sleep, we said goodbye to our good friends, and by "our good friends," I'm referring to the comfortable real bed and the warm house. We shoved our stuff back into the car (picture a Japanese subway), and headed southeast to the Sierra Nevada mountains. Ominous storm clouds gathered as we approached the foothills, but the weather was fine.

Five hours later, we arrived at our secluded campsite in the Azalea campground of the King's Canyon National Park. It was wonderful in spite of the snow.

The first order of business was to pull out the laptop and update the journal.

Lena allowed me to choose this campsite only after I assured her that it wouldn't be colder to be right next to the snow.

We were 6,500 feet above sea level. The airbed inflated without problems and we had three sleeping bags for the two of us. A warm and cozy night awaited us.

OK, the laptop in the snow was the part that I made up (I did warn you that this story would only be "mostly true"). We are actually doing our picture uploading and journal writing in the posh John Muir lodge here at King's Canyon National Park (I also made up the part about going to a rave). We hiked over from the campsite carrying our laptop cases like a couple of business persons.

Let me take a moment to tell you how much I like Gunilla, our GPS device. A GPS car device was relatively new to a tightwad like me, and this was our first trip with one. I'm embarrassed that we've given a name to the GPS. It's disgustingly cutesy to name a device, but a talking GPS is different. We had to name her. My laptop, Larry, agrees. Gunilla's a little quirky at times, as you'll see, but she gets the job done.

Note that if you do name devices, and I'm not recommending it, the rule is that the name and the device name start with the same sound. Thus, Marty the Meat Thermometer, or Cecil the Circular Saw.

After web surfing in the lodge, I considered going for a bike ride, but there were no showers around, and the shoulders of the roads were narrow. Either that or I just didn't feel like it.

We headed back and cooked up a healthful meal of macaroni and cheese with hot dogs.

We finished off the meal with some ElderTang (that is, orange-flavored Metamucil), then sat in front of the fire inhaling smoke.

CHAPTER NINE
ZERO DARK HUNDRED

May 3, 2009—Sequoia to Tehachapi: This was an interesting day—with a surprise or two.

It's weird to be writing this journal while on the trip. We're partly on a trip, and partly writing about a trip (and right now I'm writing about writing about the trip), and it reminds me of a New Yorker cartoon showing people at a party. A guy with a video camera announces "OK, everybody. Now it's time to watch the video of the first half of the party!"

That's how it is on this trip: we do stuff and then I write about it. Two other things to note: What we choose to do is influenced by how it will affect the journal ("Gotta camp by the snow 'cause it will make a killer photo for the journal!"). The other thing is that when I wake up at night, I can't get back to sleep because I'm working on composing the next entries in my head. The sentence that you're reading right now was composed at 3:17 AM.

This day started at Zero-Dark-Hundred. I've finally arranged my life so that I can sleep as late as I want, and I struggle to sleep until 5 AM. In my teens and twenties, I could easily sleep 9-10 hours per night.

For one year, in grad school, I decided I just didn't have time for all that silly sleeping stuff. I vowed that I would only sleep eight hours per night, and each night I'd set the alarm for eight hours from the time I went to bed. I'm pretty sure that policy resulted in permanent brain damage.

Just as the sun was starting to warm us up, it was time to pack up and continue on. When packed, the trunk of the Echo looks a can of sardines.

Many owners of huge SUVs are surprised that we can fit all our camping, biking, and general items into such a small car, but it's really not that difficult, especially if you can use the whole rear seat area. On trips made after this one, I hit upon the trick of removing the rear seat, which adds even more space.

The number one aggravation on a trip like this, without question, involves searching for things. If the sardine you want is at the bottom, or if you aren't sure where it is, you're in for some grief. It helps to have strict rules about where you put things, but "where the heck is the flashlight" moments are inevitable.

The route out of King's Canyon and through Sequoia was fantastic. This photo shows the road at the start of our descent from the mountains.

I kept thinking how much fun this descent would be on my bike. There is a macho cyclist rule: "Thou must not ride down the mountain unless thou hast ridden up the mountain." But about halfway down, I couldn't take it anymore, macho rule or not. We pulled over and I got on the bike. Luckily Lena didn't care to ride, so she drove the sag wagon.

We set a meet-up point, Lena drove ahead, and I got seven miles of free downhill riding. I didn't go wild—max speed was only 32 MPH, but I did go faster than the cars, and the road surface was creamy smooth. Yes, I'm a cheap gravity whore.

When we met up, we were in the desert—no more mountains. We had lunch at an LA-Yuppie place with a wonderful breeze blowing through the over-arching trees. Luckily, the crow poop landed on our table just *before* the omelet arrived.

After lunch, heading through the orange groves southeast of Visalia, we were ready for some showers, and I don't mean the rain type. We asked Gunilla for the location of the closest community swimming pool. She found one just a few miles away, and gave us the phone number, but a quick call told us that the pool was closed on Sundays. Is it me, or is it strange to close a pool on Sunday, when kids are off from school?

Speaking of Gunilla, she has a sick sense of humor, and loves to suggest we drive on dirt roads. Sometimes she doesn't realize that two roads that are close to one another aren't necessarily connected. Another quirk is that she doesn't like U-turns. If you miss a turnoff, she'll take you a mile out of your way to get back on the correct route rather than suggest you make a U-turn and go to the best road. I think she was a lawyer in another life, and is concerned about liability.

We stocked up on groceries in Bakersfield, and filled up the gas tank. I was disappointed to find that with all the steep mountain driving and the loaded car, we'd only gotten 28 MPG. Normally on a trip we'll get over 40. Hopefully with flatter driving later we'll do better.

We checked out another pool in Arvin, CA (a few miles from Bakersfield), but it was also closed. We gave up on pools and made the left turn towards St. Louis. It was at this point that we started climbing out of the central valley towards the Tehachapi pass. These transitions are great: one minute you're on pancake-flat, arrow-straight roads, and the next you're climbing into the foothills, with the loaded Echo straining.

The weather was great with hefty clouds forming over the mountains. As we came to the exit for the town of Tehachapi, we saw a sign for "Indian Hill Campground," and took the exit. After some searching, and a stop to get a phone book, we called and found out what I knew but had forgotten: "Campground" no longer means "campground." It now means "RV Park." As in "big parking lot with no tents allowed."

So it was back to the freeway where we discovered a sign that said "Entrance ramp closed." It was indeed coned off. This was a surprise, and there was no explanation or suggested alternate route. This is an area where it may be 20 miles between entrance ramps. But our road atlas showed another ramp three miles to the east, and we headed to that one.

To set the scene, I'll note that the wind was screaming. I'd guess the wind-speed was a steady 55 MPH from the west, with higher gusts.

We get to the next entrance, and find that it is also closed. We also notice that there are no cars on the freeway—something is going on here. We found out later that one of the wind turbines blew over onto the freeway. That gives you an idea of how hard it was blowing.

So we follow the traffic along a detour route through the hills. It's about 4 PM at this point, and Lena's keen eye picks out a sign for a Kern County campground. After eight miles of driving up some narrow and steep roads, we indeed found the Tehachapi Mountain Park. A big sign at the entrance told us "Do Not Cut on Trees," and we figured we could live with that, so we pulled in and found a great spot. The place was deserted.

The wind was still howling, and much gustier here. There was no way to have any kind of cooking fire, so our dinner consisted of Goober PBJ sandwiches and raw vegetables with spray on salad dressing.

If you've seen video of tents pitched on Everest, that's what ours looked like. This was one of the only times I've actually staked down the tent. Being inside, it felt as though an ogre periodically grabbed it and shook it. It was cold also—colder than the site next to the snow.

The airbed was terrific and we slept in total comfort. The inside of the tent was cozy, with a faux-flannel sleeping bag spread over the mattress with our two down sleeping bags on top.

The mattress inflated in a minute or two with the four-D-cell pump. Because the pump (Peter the Pump) was so important (the airbed is not inflatable by mouth), we treated it like Monty Python's holy hand grenade. It had its own box with ample padding, and it lived in the most protected area of the car.

The winds rocked us to sleep, and we woke refreshed.

CHAPTER TEN
MEET OUR BIKES

This chapter is for fellow cyclists who are interested in what bikes we're riding. Not you? Then you won't miss anything by skipping ahead.

I was pretty worried about bicycle thieves taking our bikes off the car when at a rest stop or in a restaurant. Then I took a look, and realized that our classic bikes, to most people, looked pretty ordinary—junkie even. I worried less at that point, but I always lock the bikes to the car with a cable that's locked to the rear towing ring. This has the advantage that if the rack were to fall off, we'd drag the bikes behind the car as if we were just married.

Thieves will steal any bike if it's easy to take. A friend put a rusty old bike in his yard for decoration. Someone stole it.

Bottecchia: I bought my Bottecchia ("Bo-take-ee-ya") in 1991, right after the fire that destroyed all our possessions (see the Everything Burned chapter). When replacing everything you own, you tend to buy things quickly (I'll take that, and that, and that), but I lucked out with this purchase. Here it is:

To riders who appreciate vintage Italian steel, it's a classic.

By the way, if you are reading this book on an electronic device, you may be able to view images full-screen. You tap, or double-tap, or click, or clap, or something. Check your device's manual to learn how to do it.

Ironman Centurion: Lena's bike is a classic also, a Dave Scott Ironman Centurion manufactured in 1987. We found it on Craigslist, after searching for months.

We loved these bikes, but I sold both of them (sniff, sniff) because we live in a very humid, salty-air climate, and I just couldn't keep ahead of the rust. Our new bikes are both aluminum.

Chapter Eleven
Al Gets a Tattoo

May 4, 2009—Tehachapi to Vegas: This was the day for us to transition from a cold, desolate mountain campsite to the glitz, the glamour, and the $10 cranberry martinis of Las Vegas.

Our day started at 6 AM with a howling wind still shaking the tent. In the morning I noticed that I'd tattooed my pants with a grease-stain image of my bike's chainring while opening the trunk with the bikes attached (it's possible, but stressful for the trunk). Note to self: Next time, get a roof rack.

We did a quick breakdown and pack up and had Gunilla lead us into Tehachapi's ultimate small-town locals coffee shop. Great service and good food.

The current owners purchased it in 1952, three weeks before it was destroyed by the Tehachapi earthquake, and then rebuilt it.

We had a good tailwind as we headed through the pass. In classic cowboy-style desert at this point, we were literally counting the miles to the first rest area which had (heavenly choir music here) showers! We hadn't bathed for a few days of gritty grimy smokey camping, and were Jonesing for some clean up (especially Lena).

Today, most Americans crave a shower after only a day or two of not bathing, but it hasn't always been that way. Prior to the fifth century or so, bathing was common in public baths. However, because the baths were often associated with prostitution and general debauchery, the Christian church blew a whistle and said "OK, everybody out of the pool!"

In addition, medical authorities of the time warned that water on the skin let diseases in. So lower class citizens essentially stopped bathing altogether, while the rich guys bathed only a few times a year. King Louis XIV of France and Queen Isabel I of Spain each bathed only twice in their lives.

It wasn't until the 1900s that the doctors said "Well, um, we take it back. We should have said bathing *prevents* disease, not *causes* it." But in the early 1900s, people still bathed only once per week. So why is it that after missing only a day or two of showering, we start to crave it so much? It's probably psychological. A few times I've said, "I sure feel grungy 'cause I haven't showered for a few days," then I'll remember that I did, in fact, just take a shower. I then feel fresh and clean again.

When we got to this magical rest area that had showers, it was closed. Lena had a lot to say about this, and it was cute since she's never really gotten the hang of swearing in English. Her swearing consists of all the bad English words she knows strung together, including the words "fart" and "throw up."

After a nice napinator nap, Lena recovered from her annoyance, and we finally came to a nice rest area which, although it didn't have showers, allowed us to clean up. We fired up the Pepsi can stove for some stir-fry chicken.

Gunilla then took our hands and led us right to the door of the Sahara hotel and casino in Vegas. Our room was only $24 ($36 with all the sneaky add-on fees and taxes). If the newest hotel were Angelina Jolie, this hotel would be Joan Rivers, with a little Carrot Top thrown in. I guess that's what you'd expect from something that was built in 1952. We had to wait in a long line to check in, the service was mediocre, and the rooms were "faded," but boy, was it great to take a long shower.

I carried the bikes in one at a time using the old "walk with purpose, look like you know what you are doing, don't make eye contact" trick. I had no idea whether bikes were allowed in the rooms, and I didn't want to find out. Since then we've often taken our bikes into hotels, and no one has ever objected.

It's actually a pretty long trek from four levels up in the garage, down the elevator, then through the casino and lobby, and up 22 levels in the hotel elevator. Multiple trips were necessary. Score some points for camping.

After sampling the exercise room on the 27th floor, we took a dip in the warmest pool I've ever encountered. It wasn't refreshing, but if it was good enough for the Rat Pack, it was good enough for me.

We'd planned to pick up some coupon books which essentially allow you to do some gambling with other people's money. For example, you can use a match play coupon to get an additional $10 when you win. So, Lena could play odd on the roulette and I could play even, so we'd make at least $10.

However, we were told that because of traffic, we didn't have time to drive the 10 blocks to the coupon place before 5 PM, and that we couldn't walk there. So we didn't do any gambling.

I've found that "walking" is a foreign concept to most Americans. The average human walking speed is 3.1 MPH, meaning it takes 20 minutes to walk a mile. Ask for directions to someplace that's a mile away, however, and you'll invariably get the response, "Oh, you're walking? Oh no, no, no, you can't *walk* there." Unfortunately, often they're right, not because it's too far, but because the roads are just unwalkable: narrow, debris-filled shoulders that make passing motorists say "Oh, look at that poor homeless man."

After another shower, we got dressed up like tourists, and headed down to "the strip." If you picture elegant people walking around town having fun gambling, then you have the wrong channel. Mostly what you see are overweight tourists from Milwaukee in shorts and dark socks sitting in a trance in front of slot machines.

You see some movie-star types, but so few that when they appear you say "Wow, look at that!"

We had a great dinner at Circus Circus and watched a pathetic ten-minute circus act consisting of a girl hanging from, and messing around in, a hula-hoop. She was very good, but there's only so much you can do hanging from a hula hoop. She was accompanied by a keyboard player and drummer who seemed disappointed with the direction their musical careers had taken. Over 150 people wanted us to see all-day presentations on time shares in exchange for a free show. No thanks.

We probably walked four miles altogether. It was less glamorous and flashy than I'd expected. I'd wanted to be overwhelmed with the waste of electricity of the flashing lights. But Lena enjoyed it, and it fulfilled her need to "see Vegas."

We headed back to the hotel and promptly fell asleep.

CHAPTER TWELVE
BAD NEWS BRAIN TUMOR

A few years before this trip, Lena was having really bad headaches. After a brain scan the doctor told us:

"Well, I have some bad news, some worse news, and some great news …"

I looked at him and frowned. "Is a good news/bad news joke really the best way to communicate this?"

"The bad news," (he ignored me), "is that your wife has a golf-ball-sized tumor in her brain, and the worse news is that that's not the cause of the headaches."

"I'm glad there's some great news, what's the great news?"

"The great news is that I have a date with my sexy receptionist tonight!"

Ha ha. No, of course it didn't actually go like that. In fact the doctor kept being vague until he made the mistake of having me drive over and pick up the latest brain scans. As soon as I got them in my hands, I pulled out the images, and using my neuroscience background and knowledge gained from reruns of *General Hospital*, I concluded that my wife had a golf-ball-sized tumor in her brain.

The doctors dug out the tumor (a "subependymoma"), and months later we discovered that the true cause of the headaches: Blood in her brain was ignoring the "One Way, Do Not Enter" sign on a vein. More sophisticated brain surgery at UCSF, and Lena was good to go.

She's actually a little different since the operations. I don't mean that she now answers to "Ralphie," she's just a little nicer and not quite so Type A. It's like I got a new wife without all the complications of a divorce.

She's also spatially challenged. We discovered this when Lena, Jenny, and I were leaving a restaurant, and Lena was heading into a closet.

"Where you goin', Babe?" I asked (No, I don't really call her "Babe").

She was embarrassed about it, so she confabulated, and said "I was looking for the dinner mints." So now, "Looking for the mints" is the code we use to refer to her spatial issues. For example, if Lena gets lost, and Jenny asks where Mom is, I'll say "She's looking for the mints."

Something I learned from this experience, involving five operations and lots of time in the ICU, is that (and write this down because it will be on the test): *Your worry level is related to the first derivative of your circumstances*. That is, it's related to the slope of the function of Circumstance Favorability versus Time.

For you non-overeducated people, I mean that your worry level is tied not to your circumstances, but to *changes* in your circumstances.

For example, your worry level is chugging along at the level that's normal for you, say a 5 on a scale from 1 to 10. You find that your wife has a brain tumor and it shoots up to 10/10. But after a while, even though your wife still has the tumor, it settles down to a 5/10 again. In other words, you adapt to your new circumstances—your new normal. Then they operate successfully, and your worry level goes down to 1/10 (Yay!). But after a while, it will drift back up to 5/10.

Patrick McManus, author of such highbrow books as *The Night the Bear Ate Goombaw*, put it this way: You always keep your worry box full. If something really bad happens, you empty out the small things, and put that big thing in it. If that big thing gets resolved, you dump it out, and fill up the box again with smaller worries.

You generally have a set worry level (or a set happiness level), and when things happen, that level will change for a while, but generally return to its regular set point. This is a valuable life lesson; it's good to know that when something bad happens, you will probably regain your former contentedness level, even if things don't improve.

The only problem I have with this idea is that, if true, there's no point in trying to better your situation. You may as well just get a bottle of vodka and hang out in the gutter, because your level of happiness/worry is going to be the same no matter what you do. Someday I will have to test that out.

CHAPTER THIRTEEN
A BIG WIN IN VEGAS!

May 6, 2009—Vegas to Zion: We were going to walk somewhere for breakfast, but I realized it would be simpler (and cheaper) to have some granola from the car. So I brought up the cereal and milk, and we had a wonderful meal in our faded hotel room.

I then worked a bit on the journal. Since Wi-Fi is $12.99 at the hotel (in Vegas, it's all about money), I just worked offline—writing the text and editing the photos.

It was lunch time when we checked out and drove off, and Lena noticed an appealing billboard for a 1 pound NY Strip steak dinner at Terrible's Casino. We dropped in, and split it. A great lunch!

Like hillbilly tourists from West Virginia, we'd so far avoided all of this immoral (at least in the Tightwad church) gambling stuff, but on the menu was an application for the gambler's club, which came with $5 of free slot machine play. You also got a free T-shirt for signing up. "Hey," I thought, "What a perfect graduation gift for Jenny!"

So we signed up and headed to the casino.It turned out that I had to add $1 of our own money to start playing, so I bit the bullet and put the money in and made all the maximum bets until the free $5 was used up.

It turns out I have a great talent for the gambling thing, and I ended up with $7.15 (a 715% profit). Instead of sinking the rest of our dough into the machines, we cashed out and got out of town. I wonder how many gamblers leave Vegas with this kind of windfall?

More praise for Gunilla: We needed a library for internet access, and an auto parts store for some "Heet" (alcohol that we use for the Pepsi can stove—see the chapter entitled "Pepsi Cooking"). We just told her what we wanted and she took us there.

Next it was 75 MPH most of the way to Zion. Great desert driving, with an interesting change at Springfield. As we approached the town, a ridge of abrupt hills made an apparently impenetrable wall that the freeway seemed destined to crash into. At the last minute, a crack in the wall became visible, and the freeway squeezed through it. A very neat thing.

We arrived at Zion National Park at about 6:30 PM and were surprised to find that all the campsites were taken, even though it was a Wednesday. However, the ranger let us stay in one of the group sites with three other sets of campers. This turned out fine, as there was plenty of room, and we had a dramatic view of the surrounding cliffs.

The temperature was somewhere between 85 and 95 degrees, which is above the maximum operating temperature for Swedes born in Jokkmokk, but it cooled fast, and there was a delicious breeze.

For dinner, we cooked the freeze-dried chicken stew which had literally been in our closet at home for 10 years. Coincidentally, it was set to expire on May 9, 2009. It was as delicious as the breeze.

The temperature was now perfect, and we had a cozy night, sleeping from about 10 PM to 7:15 AM. I woke at 3 AM to hear a strong wind and what sounded like rain. In the morning we determined that it was tent catepillars dropping on the tent.

CHAPTER FOURTEEN
AL CRASHES

May 6, 2009—Zion to Zion: This day included an incredible ride and a bike crash!

We packed up the car and got ready for our ride up Zion canyon. This is a ride that all cyclists should put on their bucket lists. You can't beat the scenery, the road is smooth, and there are very few cars (cars are prohibited for most of it).

The start of the ride was on a bike/pedestrian trail. We were going to skip that, figuring that the trail would be clogged with tourists. Not so—it was deserted.

This is where the "Wow" and "I can't believe it" part started. Every turn had more fantastic, huge cliffs to see.

It was only 8 miles to the Temple of Sinwava at the top end of the canyon, and when we arrived, we walked on a trail for another mile or so. As I mentioned, this route is closed to cars. The only way to see it is walking, on bike, or on a shuttle or tour bus.

On the way down we were being passed by a tour bus, and I decided to stop on the shoulder. However it turned out the shoulder was much softer than I expected. I watched as my front tire dug in, and the bike and I rotated around it. I came this close [indicates tiny distance with fingers] to hitting some big rocks, and landed pretty well, due to dumb luck, with no damage to the bike.

I had scrapes and bruises at around eight places on my bod, and the camera (back pocket) was a little damaged. This photo shows both my injuries and the camera's. That is, the little shutter in front of the lens doesn't always open now. But we're both improving and functioning well.

We had such a great time here that we decided to do it again the next day.

I've got some fun things to come: Mennonite women playing softball in the hot sun with full length dresses and bonnets, war driving in Bryce, Arches National Park, and coconut cream pie. But first, here's one of those "sidebar" chapters.

CHAPTER FIFTEEN
CRASHES—CYCLING'S DARK SIDE

I often think about crashing. More at night than when riding. In bed, the idea of riding on the freeway with a 70 MPH, 40-ton logging truck three feet from my elbow is troubling. When I'm on the bike, however, it seems a lot tamer.

But even without "cagers" (that is, car and truck drivers) crashing is an issue you have to consider.

I've fallen a few times. I was riding over a frozen foot/bike bridge in Michigan, and I was thinking, will I fall if I put on the brakes? I couldn't resist trying it, touched the brakes, and down I went. So I got the answer to my question: yes.

When I first tried clip-in pedals (aka clipless pedals), I stopped on the shoulder, my feet remained stuck to the pedals, and I fell neatly into the #2 lane of the California 101 freeway. It almost became the #2 lane, literally. Don't picture a Los Angeles freeway, there are many fewer cars here. With some bad luck, however, I would have checked in to Motel Deep Six.

My worst crash happened in a pace-line (cyclists riding close to one another in a line to reduce wind resistance) during the Wildflower century. The guy in front of me slowed, and all the dominoes went down. I was out of the cycling business for a month or two.

But the crash that made me reconsider cycling as a hobby was Lena's major mishap on a bicycle path in Redding, California. The curves on this hilly section of the trail were much sharper than those you find on a regular road. Think about it, a path can have a turn with a radius of only 20 feet.

Lena was riding 30 seconds ahead of me. I came around a curve, and found her on the ground, bloody and not moving. You can see where this happened in this picture that displays the data from my GPS cyclocomputer. She was coming downhill from the top of the picture, and I found her at the yellow X.

I thought she was just resting after being shaken up. No, she was AWOL. Her bike was on top of her. I called for an ambulance, but it was hard to describe to them exactly where we were, I ended up giving them the latitude and longitude from my cyclocomputer.

The lights gradually came on, but there was still nobody home. She kept asking the same questions over and over. Her helmet was cracked.

I finally heard the ambulance chugging up the bike path after 30 minutes. Apparently this didn't qualify for using the siren or driving fast. I thought it was pretty serious, but what do I know, I'm not a lawyer.

At the hospital we found that she had five cracked and broken ribs, scraped pizza here and there, and no other broken bones. All of those things were serious, but not worrisome. The worrisome part, and the part that made me reconsider cycling, was the bleeding on the brain (subarachnoid hemorrhage). The docs put her in the ICU, and told me that if the bleeding, causing an increase in intracranial pressure, didn't stop by morning, they would have to drill a hole in her skull.

The bleeding did stop in time to avoid surgery, and it turns out that having the prior brain tumor operation may have helped out here. Lena has a big square "trap door" bone flap in her skull from that earlier repair job, held in place by scar tissue. It expanded outward a bit, possibly helping to relieve pressure.

When considering whether riding is worth the risk, you might say "Well, everything has its dangers. You can't live your life in fear. And being a couch potato is dangerous to your health." Little phrases like that are just glib ways of avoiding a very difficult decision. When you are in the ICU wondering whether your wife will live or die, the risks are much less abstract. In other words, in the ICU with the machines, tubes, and smells, you say "I don't want this to ever happen again. I don't care about the probabilities."

And of course it could have been much worse. Members of bikeforums.net talk about being in comas, or having permanent deficits, but still riding.

Lena vowed never to ride again, and I was thinking along the same lines, but as time separates us from the experience, we move back to the "Just do it!" philosophy. We did buy new helmets, the best we could find— POC Trabec Race helmets with MIPS protection.

One friend, when I talked about never riding again, said "It doesn't have to be an all or nothing thing. You can just decide to ride on less dangerous roads." He's right, and that's good advice, but I reminded him that this happened on a tame bike/pedestrian path.

Lena still doesn't remember the crash. Our guess is that she was going a little too fast for the curve, and slid on some gravel, using her ribs to break her fall.

The bleeding on the brain stopped, and she made a full recovery. She was released after two days. I asked one doctor whether he thought the bill would exceed our $7,000 deductible. He got a good laugh out of that. The total bill was $145,000.

CHAPTER SIXTEEN
WAR DRIVING

May 7, 2009—Zion to Bryce: Because yesterday's ride was the most dramatic of our lives, we listened to the philosophers Captain and Tenille and told Zion "Do that to me one more time." It's nice to be able to wake up and say "What shall we do today?"

After we got back, it was time to move on to Bryce. Because both nights at Zion saw us getting the last available campsite, the "find a site" stress level was raised significantly. Getting to campgrounds early had become a high priority.

We stopped at the Thunderbird Lodge in Carmel Junction (super small town), and had perhaps the best service we've ever received. Everyone who worked at this place was having a great time, and we rewarded them by ordering a coconut cream pie to split for dessert. This is my new favorite pie flavor. [Ah, the memories of our high-carb days …]

We arrived at Bryce at three in the afternoon, got in free with our National Park Annual Pass, and chose (again!) one of the last remaining campsites. We left one of our bags at the table to reserve the site, registered, and then went to take a peek at the canyon.

As mentioned, the most difficult thing about traveling with everything in the tiny Echo is the problem of finding stuff. The trunk is inaccessible when the bikes are on the rack, and we've learned what needs to live in the passenger compartment. We enforce our "no stuff left behind" policy by making a CDO sweep of every campsite when leaving (CDO is OCD but with the letters in their proper, alphabetical order—OCD is Obsessive-Compulsive Disorder). So we are confident that what we're seeking is "in there somewhere." But sometimes things just disappear.

One of those times came at the Bryce visitor's center. I needed the "Al's Cold Weather Clothes" bag, and we just couldn't find it. We pretty much took everything out of the car, unloaded the bikes, and pulled out our hair until Lena remembered that that was the bag we'd put on the table at the campsite to reserve it.

Another example is the ElderTang. It's missing. We have not been able to find it. We know it's around somewhere, but it's been AWOL since Zion day one. That could put a crimp in our style.

Back to the narrative: there were trails down into the canyon, but for us, those would have to wait until tomorrow, since it was getting late.

The wind was still rioting, and at 8,000 feet above sea level, the temperature headed south as the afternoon wore on. I was able to shield the dinner fire somewhat, but it was still a blast furnace. The burgers were charred on the outside, red on the inside, and, like, totally good. What's black and red and good all over? Blast-furnace burgers.

The urge to upload our recent photos grew, and there was no Wi-Fi at the lodge, so it was time for some war-driving—that is, looking for unguarded, unsecured Wi-Fi hotspots. We soon found one outside the "High Plains Institute." Actually, we think this was a public spot, so we weren't criminals after all.

An indispensable part of our equipment was the inverter that lets us get 110 AC from the car. Thus we can charge up or run the computers, charge batteries for walkie-talkies and flashlights, as well as refresh the cell phone and Gunilla. Everyone has to take turns however, flashlights one day, computers the next, etc.

Stay tuned for Lena's destruction of a national monument.

CHAPTER SEVENTEEN
LENA BREAKS A NATIONAL MONUMENT

May 8, 2009—Bryce to Arches: Another icy morning here at 8,000 feet. I always try to get the coffee started before Lena wakes up. She usually appreciates this. However, I did this in Vegas by going down to the Starbucks and bringing her a cup while she was still sleeping. "Where's the stirrer?" she said. But *usually* she appreciates it.

The fire was started with some nice dry wood that we brought from Zion. The menu was scrambled eggs, lightly charred whole wheat toast, coffee, hot cocoa, and OJ.

The eggs were scrambled in one of our disposable frying pans. Yes, I said "disposable." Here's the great tip: Before you go on a car camping trip, pick up a bunch of pots and pans from garage sales. Where we live you can get them for 25 cents each. Pan gets charred on the bottom because you're cooking on a wood fire? Food sticks to the pan? Who cares? Use it and lose it. This is much better than crouching by a icy faucet scrubbing away. Is it environmentally wasteful? Yes, but most of those pans wouldn't have found a new home anyway.

Another tip: Use Egg Beaters type egg substitutes when camping. They taste almost as good as real eggs, but they don't break. I'd much rather have a real egg, but sifting egg yolks out of the cooler water is no fun.

After breakfast we did a quick hike down into the canyon. We wanted to get on our way quickly, because it was a Friday, and we figured that campsites would go fast at Arches National Park, our next stop. Little did we know, but they were already all taken by 7:30 AM. It would have been nice to call ahead and ask "When do you think the campground will fill up?" However, if you call the Arches number you get "Press 1 for

52

English, press 2 for Spanish" and it's all downhill from there. That is, you generally can't get through to a real person. Permit me to dream about how it would be in an ideal world, with a genuine human answering the phone:

"Hi, Arches National Park, this is Shirley."
"Yes, we'll be driving in this afternoon, will the campsites fill up by then?"
"Let me check … Yes, I'm sorry, they will all be taken, but Fred's campground up the road will have sites available. His number is 555-1234"
"OK, thanks!"

Automated telephone menus are great for companies, but lousy for customers. The main reason is that speech is slow. If you have three menus with 10 options each, it takes forever to get through them. Plus, you have to "Listen carefully because menu options have changed." Here's a solution: you go on a company's web site and make your selections there. The site gives you an extension number, you call the company, and punch in the extension number. With thousands skipping the slow phone menu, hold times would be significantly reduced.

And could we all sign an agreement saying we realize that "Your call may be recorded or monitored for quality assurance"? Then we could skip that, and save the millions of hours of productivity that are wasted listening to those announcements.

OK, and here's another message to companies: When you put us on hold, perhaps we'd like to do some work. We may have to sit for 10 minutes, and we might like to check email or do some writing. So don't interrupt the music every 20 seconds with advertisements ("Did you know that you can save 10% if you sign up for …").

So, rants over, back to our hike. It was cold but heating up fast as we descended into the canyon. Bryce is "HooDoo" central (Googleimage it). They are formed because different rock layers erode at different rates. With a resistant layer on the top, a hoodoo forms. This is the same principle governing Bruce Jenner's plastic surgery.

The bottom of the canyon was fascinating, and worth the climb down. We would have enjoyed a longer hike—maybe next year.

After the hike we went to the lodge where I played the piano to keep my hand in. It was horribly out of tune, and Ab above middle C was missing, so I just played one song and left.

It was at this point in the trip that we looked at our progress on the map, and realized we had better get our happy asses in gear if we were going to arrive in St. Louis on the 13th. We had thought to visit Canyonlands, Capitol Reef, and/or Escalante, but instead went right to Arches.

We arrived at the entrance station at around 3 PM, only to be told that the campground had filled up early in the morning. They gave us a list of other campground possibilities. So we worked our way through these very nice campgrounds, each with 3 to 19 campsites, located right on the Colorado River. It wasn't an easy process, since the windy road was narrow, and checking a campground consisted of driving on bumpy dirt roads and looking at the tags on each site. We repeated this process at 7-10 campgrounds, until we were about 30 miles from Arches. Neither of us cracked.

At the Hittle Bottom campground, we decided that if there were no sites, we'd continue on to Colorado. But we got the last site. We were pretty tired at this point, but figured that we'd regret it later if we didn't see Arches National Park, so after setting up the site, we drove the 30 miles back. The alternative was to sit at the campsite in the direct sun. It wasn't too hot, maybe 80, and it was a dry heat. But still.

So, back to the park it was. Pictures don't do these structures justice, of course. The hoodoos are huge and weird. My favorites are the gigantic, narrow wall-type structures.

This next shot is of a hoodoo called "Balanced Rock." The shock waves from Lena's crunchy apple caused the hoodoo to become "unbalanced rock."

This was terribly embarrassing, so we lowered our heads and got out of there fast.

Next, back to our campsite for a cold beer. There was an actual cowboy herding cattle while we did this. I'm 90% sure that it is not something that they stage just for the tourists.

At first sight, the campsite appeared barren and exposed. But it was just perfect for experiencing the feeling of this big-sky kind of place. You don't get that driving through.

As soon as the sun went behind the cliff, it got even more pleasant. We had the second pair of hamburgers for dinner, and they were just as good as the charred/raw burgers from Bryce. We would have to atone tomorrow for our three burger meals in a row. The Eldertang is still missing.

CHAPTER EIGHTEEN
MEET MY MOM

My mom, like everyone in my family, was a character, but much more idealistic and impetuous than I am. Artistic, creative, and dramatic are adjectives that would describe her. Pragmatic, down-to-earth, cautious—not so much.

People like that are more likely to have amusing mishaps. For instance, if you put on a bikini and paint yourself from head to toe with gold spray paint from the hardware store for a Goldfinger Halloween costume (sister #2), you might win a ride in an ambulance. If you use glue to give yourself spiky hair for funny-hairdo-day (sister #1), you'll have an amusing anecdote about the spiky hairdo that wouldn't go away.

Here's an example of my mom's impulsiveness. When sister #3 was getting married in Douglas, Arizona, a potent norovirus swept through the wedding party. This illness made the black death seem like mild sniffles, and came on quickly.

The night before her planned drive back to San Diego, my mom started feeling sick. She knew what was coming, but instead of the practical choice of waiting to see how bad it would be, or waiting until she recovered, she threw all her stuff in the car at midnight and started on the seven-hour trip home. The result was an entertaining story about the nightmare car drive from hell. In addition, it had slipped her mind that we had some more wedding events the next morning. The bride was not pleased.

My point is that careful people have fewer adventures. Whether this is good or bad depends on your point of view. You want adventures like this? Just be less cautious. The most entertaining adventure books start with sentences like this: "I set off on my around-the-world solo trip having been on a sailboat only twice in my life."

I've had to work hard all my life to compensate for my inherited "Spacey Macy" tendencies. I depend on checklists and unbreakable rules such as "don't put anything on the roof of the car, even for a second." Once, as a musician, I said to myself, "I'm tired of being so careful all the time. Musicians are carefree, maybe in my musician life I'll be less careful." When I was late for a concert, and had to walk out on stage after the first number and squeeze in between the other trombones, I went back to being careful.

When my mom announced that she would drive across the country alone with her 11- and 14-year-old children (my parents were divorced), most people thought that was reckless. Mom's response was, "Oh, don't be silly, it will be fine." My 14-year-old self agreed with her, but I realize now that when you are an adult with two kids and a sketchy car, you don't have much margin for error.

For example, our car broke down in Oklahoma on the side of the highway. A truck overflowing with rough-looking migrant workers stopped to help us, and my mom sent me off with them to bring back help. It turned out fine, but she later told me she was worried she'd never see me again.

The other mishap on this trip happened near Deming, New Mexico. In a thunderstorm, we found ourselves searching for an elusive campground. As we got further from civilization, the road (the correct one?) got muddier until finally we could go no farther. It was late at night, so Mom decided we should sleep in the car, and head back in the morning. We moved boxes around to give us enough room to sleep. This plan would have worked, except that one of the boxes rested against the brake pedal, turning on the brake lights, and resulting in a dead battery come morning.

We woke in a huge muddy field in the pouring rain, and one of us had to go for help. This time it was my mom that made the trip, and she returned several hours later riding on the back of a bulldozer. We got the car out, and resumed our trip. It wasn't really that dangerous, but it was an adventure that wouldn't have happened without the idealistic decision to make a somewhat risky trip.

I'm probably a more interesting person due to this upbringing, given that I didn't end up as a slave in a migrant worker camp.

CHAPTER NINETEEN
PICKING UP HITCHHIKERS

May 9, 2009—Arches to Loma: I woke up at about 5:30 AM, took a look around the desert sky and saw Mars rising in the east. It looked like a small version of the moon, while at the same time, the moon itself was setting behind a cliff in the west.

Each day we discover a few hitchhikers—that is, caterpillars who have cocooned themselves onto our belongings and various body parts. Little, sticky cotton-ball mementos of our time in Zion.

Since this was a Saturday, we knew we might have trouble finding a site at the next campground, so we got on the road by about 6:30 AM. We hit the tail end of the cow commute (tail end, get it?), and had to wait for some of them to clear the road.

Many of the telephone poles here have perches above the wires so that the large birds won't land between the wires and electrocute themselves, so we got to see several non-fried golden eagles.

After breakfast at Starvin' Arvin's, near Fruita, we went to the Colorado welcome center, and asked about camping. The Highline Lake State Park was only 15 miles away. We called, and were told that they had one site left (do you see a pattern here?), so we boogied on up there and grabbed it.

This place was luxury for us. 9:30 AM, after only a few hours of driving, and we already had a campsite, plus showers and a laundromat! We could get used to this. The water heater for the showers was broken (to be fixed in an hour or so), but I took a cold shower anyway because I am that macho.

We unhurriedly set up the tent on some lush grass, and then took off for a bike ride. The roads were great. Narrow shoulders, but very little traffic.

We headed to Fruita, 15 miles away, and managed to hit the one hill in the entire area, as you can see in this photo.

This was a great ride, except for one thing: flats. We got not one or two, but a total of eight flats. Four on the way to town, one on the way back, and three more that didn't manifest themselves until we took the bikes off the rack the next day. A note for you carbon dioxide cartridge elitists—if I'd had a carbon dioxide inflater with only a few cartridges, I'd have been seeing the sights of Colorado on foot. Check out the Bicycling Tips chapter for my solution to the inflater vs. pump debate.

Why so may flats? Here's why: Goathead thorns. All of the flats were caused by these little suckers. I'd never heard of them before. Spiky thorns designed by God to puncture bicycle tires. They felt like pieces of wire when I ran my finger inside the tire—that's how strong they are. If a normal thorn were Honey Boo Boo, this thorn would be the Cracken. If a normal thorn were a Cheerio, this thorn would be the planet Jupiter. If … well, you get the idea.

Anyway, in Fruita we had a great chicken/cranberry/pear/walnut/blue cheese salad with a side of pizza at the Hot Tomato Cafe.

On the way back we passed a Mennonite softball game. There were women playing in full dresses and bonnets and army boots. It was hot with a bright sun. You should see them run around the bases. I will risk going to hell by saying, "This is one goofy-assed religion."

When we got back to the campsite, it was time for some luxurious showers, with hot water. Four quarters for four minutes of heaven.

We needed to do some stocking up, so we asked Gunilla the GPS about grocery stores, and selected a Safeway in Grand Junction. She took us there via a strange backroads route, but it may have been the best way. Before we started shopping, we wanted to update the journal and check email, so we asked for the location of a nearby coffee shop.

This was the point at which Gunilla really lost it. The first place was "Coffeetime" and she took us on a roundabout route to someone's house. I knocked on the door and asked the resident "Are you *sure* there isn't a coffee shop here, perhaps in your basement?" The answer was a definite "No!" so Gunilla got one demerit, and we next told her to take us to a Starbucks. Another convoluted route, and when Gunilla said "Arriving at Starbucks, on left" we were looking at a vacant ditch, with no buildings nearby.

We handled the situation well. We threw Gunilla into the ditch yelled at her to bring us back a latte. No, we just said "Gunilla, go to your room." Don't feel bad for her; she lives in Gunilla's Malibu Dream House—a pink plastic thermos. The thermos is a great place for her; it keeps her protected from bumps, and doesn't clue in thieves that we have an expensive, state-of-the-art, high-tech device in our car.

So we gave up on Wi-Fi and coffee (or "Whiffy" as some people around here pronounce it). Not everyone is familiar with the term "Wi-Fi." Apparently a blonde went up to the counter at a local coffee shop and asked for a Wi-Fi. When the barista looked puzzled, the blonde said "Hello!" and pointed to a sign in the window that said "Free Wi-Fi."

Back at Safeway, we were going to get some chicken pieces and firewood, and go back to the campsite and cook dinner, but then Lena had a better idea: Buy some cooked barbecued chicken. This was genius, and we had a tasty chicken and coleslaw dinner back at the site with no smoke in our eyes, plus plenty of leftover chicken for tomorrow's lunch.

Lena got the laundry started after dinner, and we decided to drive into Fruita for our Wi-Fi fix. The two coffee shops were closed, but the Hot Tomato had Wi-Fi, and although it was a loud yuppie type environment, we got our work done, and I wrote up a few days worth of journal entries.

When we returned, there was quite a party going on at the mega-accumulator's site across the way but we put in our earplugs, and went right to sleep. "Accumulator" is my term for a person who can't stop accumulating toys: big trucks, boats, big BBQs, and so on. But who's judging?

Stay tuned for sandals in the snow, but first, a more serious chapter about camping.

CHAPTER TWENTY
CAMPING IS DEAD

Let's All Mourn the Loss of Camping: Before camping died, it looked like this: A family drives a station wagon into a campground, picks out a nice site, and sets up a modest tent. The kids run off to catch bullfrogs, swim in the pond with the other kids, and engage in other Norman Rockwell type activities. After dinner, they sit around a small fire, talk quietly, listen to the crickets and the wind in the trees, and gaze at the stars. That sounds nice, doesn't it?

But that type of camping is dead because now, it's party time with as many of your toys as you can cram into your huge pickup truck and trailer, plus all the drinking buddies you can assemble! A typical campsite might have an RV, several canopy structures, two huge tents, six coolers, several gas grills, and 12 folding chairs.

A quick observation about those humongous, complicated three-or-more-room tents that are popular today: I've observed that tent setting up time is not happy family time.

The three tent stakes driven through the heart of camping are noise, light, and overcrowding.

Stake number one is noise. Sounds then: Wind in the trees, birds, crickets, happy kids. Sounds now: Car alarms, generators, boom boxes, cell phone rings, cell phone conversations, Playstation tunes, and loud drunken laughing over party music.

Before the death of camping, you might spend the afternoon in the shade of a tree with your summer reading. But now, even if the temperature is a pleasant 75 degrees, your neighbor's huge RV will be heating up like a meth lab in Bakersfield. So he or she will turn on the air conditioning, which means running the generator. All day. Instead of listening to the breeze in the trees, you're now essentially sitting next to an idling cement truck.

Worse, generators are no longer limited to RV's. Now even tent campers bring portable generators so that they can watch their favorite reality show on TV.

The constant generator hum is punctuated with car alarms. Every campground is treated to at least one car alarm per night. And since many cars and trucks have remote locks that briefly honk the horn and flash the lights when locked, your sleep is interrupted each time one of these campers visits his or her vehicle.

Stake number two is light pollution. When campers turn on their maxi-light camping lanterns each night (I'm not making this up: some even come with remote controls), the stars fade out until the sky resembles that of Times Square. It's worse, actually, because in the city, people have their lights on inside their houses, but at the campground, the lights are outside.

This doesn't bother many of the "campers," since the sunset finds them inside their RV, watching Duck Dynasty. For anyone who's experienced true wilderness, however, the great outdoors now feels like a fully lit Dodger Stadium.

The final stake in camping's heart is overcrowding. Your camping experience may actually begin at 12:00 AM on January 1, when you attempt to reserve a site at one of the more favored destinations. Some campgrounds in California are fully booked for popular summer dates by 4 AM. As population increases, we can keep building new Home Depots and strip malls, but the campgrounds are limited.

A large national reservation company may have handled your reservation. The largest booked over 4 million reservations in 2006. Instead of driving through the campground and choosing a site that is a bit away from other sites, a computer server in downtown Chicago assigns you a specific campsite.

If you camp in Yosemite Valley, you'll find that the individual sites have been squeezed together like mini tectonic plates until every square foot of space is used up. And urban sprawl is bringing new freeways right up against camping areas that were formerly in the wilderness.

I've been talking about car camping here, of course. So you might be thinking that if you want to recreate the real camping experience, all you have to do is go backpacking.

Yes, that's true in many cases, however some backpacking destinations experience so many backpackers that they now prohibit firewood collection. No cozy campfire for you. At Mount Rainier National Park, there are so many hikers, that backpackers are required to put all of their waste, and I'm not talking just about coffee grounds here, into bags and pack it out with them. You thought it was gross to pick up after your dog. Be sure you don't open the wrong stuff sack when looking for the trail mix!

Can camping be revived? I used to think that perhaps some segregated areas of campgrounds could be set up to prohibit all music, generators, and bright lanterns. But that would require a level of organization and enforcement that isn't justified by the apparently small number of campers looking for a simpler, more natural experience.

Instead, I've just come to accept that most people's idea of "roughing it" consists of television without cable. If you're looking for the pre-camping-death experience, you'll just have to camp off-season at a campground far from the major population centers, take your eye-shades, and load your music player with a recording of nature sounds.

CHAPTER TWENTY-ONE
SHORTS IN THE SNOW

May 10, 2009—Loma to Bonny Lake: We located the ElderTang! It had found its way into the adventure bag along with the blue plastic cereal bowl. Much rejoicing.

Another Zero-Dark-Hundred start—someday we're going to learn how to sleep late. The first job before heading off was to sort the clean laundry, which we did in the dark.

This had been a great "refit" stop. We were cleaned, laundered, exercised, reorganized, and rejuvenated.

Here's roll call for the bags (note that you can see Gunilla's Malibu Dreamhouse on the floor of the front seat):

Top row: Al laptop, Lena big big heavy Imelda Marcos bag, Al cold weather clothes, sleeping bags and pillows, biking bag, Al warm weather clothes, towels and sheet, tent, tent poles, cozy tent bag. Bottom row: dirty clothes, kitchen, Lena laptop, camping bag 2. Not pictured: Adventure bag (jackets and binoculars), electronics bag, chairs, toolbox, cooler, food box, frying pan bag, paper plate bag.

Segregating everything into small bags helps us find things. For example, to find the stove, we only have to find the kitchen bag, and look in it. We carefully purchased bags that had different colors to help when searching —no, wait a second, all the bags are different colors because we accumulated them over years of garage-sale shopping.

Today we followed the Colorado River through the Rockies. We'd planned to drive through Rocky Mountain National Park, but we called ahead and learned that the summit road was closed. We still planned to visit it (after all, it would be free because we had our annual pass), but as we got up in elevation, the weather turned snowy and windy, so we changed our minds.

We drove through snow squalls, and the lack of lane markers on the road (all worn away) made driving difficult (Colorado Department of Transportation, if you're reading this, try the little plastic markers that California uses).

We've done a lot of climate changing on this trip, and sometimes we end up with the wrong clothes on. Here's a driver change near the summit. You can't see it, but I'm wearing sandals and almost standing in a puddle of ice-water.

The weather was pretty bad here, so we decided to take a break and look for some Wi-Fi and coffee. We stopped in Frisco, and found a great place (Rocky Mountain Coffee Roasters). People from San Francisco hate hearing the word "Frisco," but here, Frisco is the correct and official name of the town, so "Frisco, Frisco, Frisco!"

I dove into cyberspace, got a few day's info into the journal, and when I came to the surface, it was sunny out. We took out our leftover chicken and coleslaw, I got a beer, and we dined al Frisco at 9,042 feet.

Back on the road, we saw that Vail and Breckenridge were huge, with lots of new building going on. In most places more than half of the trees were dead. The whitebark pines are being massacred by the mountain pine beetles. Milder winters and warmer summers are allowing the beetles to flourish, and 19% of the trees in Rocky Mountain National Park are infested.

We passed through Denver and on to our next campground: Bonny Lake. This place was almost deserted, and a little desolate due to the cloudy windy weather. On the menu: Baked beans and hot dogs. The coyotes sung us to sleep.

Our gas mileage has improved substantially since that first 28 MPG tank. We had a 35 MPG day, and two 39 MPG days. I keep our tires at the max pressure of 44 psi, but when I checked at Zion, they were at 50 psi due to the elevation change! Oops.

Coming up: duct tape car repairs, followed by Larry the Cable Guy and killer tornadoes in Missouri! Don't miss it.

CHAPTER TWENTY-TWO
MORE FLATS

May 11, 2009—Bonny Lake to Kanopolis: This day started with a walk to the edge of Bonny Lake. Whoops, who moved the lake? Instead there's a boat ramp to nowhere—about a half mile from the current edge of the water.

The trim over the car's wheel well had come loose a few years ago, and I had glued it back on with a hot-glue gun. This worked fine in our cool coastal climate, but it was no match for the desert. So the tip came loose, and made more noise than a Kardashian getting her back-hair waxed. This required some temporary surgery using the duct tape/WD-40 principle (if it moves and it shouldn't, fix it with duct tape. If it should move and doesn't, fix it with WD-40).

Speaking of road noise, some of the pavement in Colorado and Kansas causes an extremely annoying whine or whistling sound when you drive on it. It's like a single note on a flute played continuously. This road noise drives me up the wall, and increases my driving fatigue. I've never experienced this before, and a little research shows that the road engineers are aware of how annoying it is.

Texturing of roadway pavement surfaces is necessary to provide adequate resistance to skidding, and to allow water to escape from under tires to minimize hydroplaning. This texturing, however, has been shown to contribute to tire noise on rigid pavements. Large aggregate mixes have also been shown to increase tire noise. Studies have been conducted by other agencies to evaluate which textures provide the needed safety attributes, while reducing the noise levels or the pure tone frequencies or "whine" that are annoying to the public.

While doing the research for this book, I've come to realize that I probably suffer from this thing called "hyperacusis." According to Wikipedia, the symptoms include: "… annoyance, and general intolerance to any sounds that most people don't notice or consider unpleasant. As many as 86% of hyperacusis sufferers also have tinnitus [ringing in the ears—true for me]." The most common cause is exposure to loud sounds—think my rock band in the 60s might be relevant here?

In any case, I'm surprised that even normal people can accept this highway whine. The only advantage of this noise is that it feels so good when you finally get to a non-noisy part of the highway.

After dinner I had a bicycle flat-tire clinic, patching the two spares and the two new "garage" flats (flats that don't happen until after the ride). Several beers were required. I've debated whether listening for leaks with my ears is better than feeling for the escaping air with my lips. Listening seems to win out, since I can also feel the wind on my ears.

The tires weren't the only thing getting flats. When we went to bed it seemed that the airbed was a little softer than usual, and sure enough, at midnight we were hitting bottom. We reinflated it, and were comfortable enough until morning.

Chapter Twenty-Three
Kidnapped!

Steve Takes a Ride in the Trunk: Here's another story about the wild antics of my buddies (and me) in high school. I'm embarrassed about this joke that went a bit too far, but this is what kids do in high school, right?

You remember my best friend Steve (the drowning "joke")? This guy was as much of a character as I was. For example, in high school, he hosted an exchange student, Adriano, from Brazil. Soon after Adriano arrived, all the new exchange students were taken to another school for a question and answer session, and Steve went along because Adriano spoke very little English.

Steve was on stage with the others, and a teacher asked what country he was from. Without a second's hesitation, Steve put on a British accent, and said "England, Mum." He got the most questions, since he was the easiest to understand, and had a great time making up details about what life was like in jolly old England. Adriano had to step on the other foreign students' toes to keep them from laughing.

On April 1, 1971 Adriano asked Steve how April Fools' Day worked. "I don't understand—how do you make someone feel like an idiot?" he asked. Steve raised his index finger and said "Watch this." He called several friends, including me, and told each he was out of gas and needed a ride. We all jumped to his assistance, only to arrive at the designated spot and find: No Steve.

All there together, we realized we'd been April Fooled, and planned our retribution: Steve would have to be kidnapped and dropped off in a remote location. We drove to his house, knocked on the door and quietly told him that we were glad he'd made it home safely. And, "by the way, we've got something to show you guys. Come outside."

We grabbed Adriano and Steve, and took them over to the open trunk. Steve knew he'd get in trouble if he struggled and alerted his parents, so they got in quietly.

As soon as we drove away, the captives started bawling and banging like bears in a trap. This presented a problem for us, since we needed gas. Self-service gas stations were still years in the future, so we knew there would be an attendant involved. We waited for a lull, and, risking discovery, pulled into a Shell station. Steve and Adriano figured out what was happening, and redoubled their noisemaking efforts.

Now here's the puzzle: The attendant, an old man, shuffled over to the car and put in the gas, staring straight ahead as if nothing was going on. His head was a foot from the trunk, yet he didn't seem to register the yells that we could hear from 20 feet away. He was either deaf or assumed we were part of the Mafia. This was indeed Long Island, but we didn't look like Mafiosi. Perhaps he realized we were just kids having some fun. In any case, he took our payment without comment, and off we went.

Steve had a new strategy at this point. We heard him yell, "I am now disconnecting your taillights!" This strategy had an upside for Steve— someone, perhaps a policeman, might stop the car and not ignore the yelling coming from the trunk. There was a downside too, of course. If you're riding in a trunk, anything that increases the chance of a rear-end collision is probably a bad idea.

His scheme didn't have any effect, and we drove to Duck Island (connected to the mainland via causeway) and dropped them off on a desolate dead-end street. When I say "dropped them off," I mean "pried them loose from the car."

Heading for home, we hadn't driven 200 yards before a police car stopped us. "Did you know that your taillights are out?" he asked. We opened the trunk and puzzled over this mysterious electrical problem, all the while darting glances down the road, expecting Steve and Adriano to come screaming up the hill.

73

Luckily for us, Steve had seen the police car, and didn't want to cause the extra trouble that would come from having the law involved. More luck —the policeman accepted our promise to fix the lights, and let us go.

The kidnapees' return to civilization was a tortuous one, since they had no idea where they were, and, of course, no transportation. After a lot of walking and hitching, they arrived at my house at 4 AM. In my mostly unconscious dream state, I mistook their arrival at my bedroom window for burglars, and when I yelled and banged on the window, it shattered. No injuries, though, and when I was fully awake, I drove them home.

Here's a photo of Adriano (on the left) and Steve taken a few months after the adventure:

Fortunately, Steve was a good-natured fellow, and perhaps because he "started it," he never held the episode against us. He went on to become a prominent astrophysicist at Caltech, publishing over 200 scientific papers.

CHAPTER TWENTY-FOUR
SUPERGLUING THE CAR

May 12, 2009—Kanopolis to Arrow Rock: We once again woke up in a NASA wind tunnel, and had to keep the breakfast fire small although there was plenty of free firewood at the site. Also, the wind kept most of the heat from getting up to the grating, so I held the disposable frying pan with the eggs right down on the fire, and we had a tasty breakfast.

Today was fix-it day, and I started by gluing the trim over the Echo's front tire.

Second fixit task: Airbed. My overly sensitive hearing is usually a disadvantage, but it pays off in the leak-finding department, and I was able to locate the pinprick leak hiding on the side of the airbed. I'm not sure what made the hole, but the PVC cement and duct tape repaired it in short order.

The next item on the agenda was to visit Lindsborg, Kansas, a town devoted to Swedish stuff. Lena had been looking forward to this ever since a bike forumite recommended it. Unfortunately, the place was a little depressing because, due to the recession, it was a ghost town. It reminded me of a science fiction movie in which all the residents of the town have mysteriously disappeared. Lena proclaimed the food 70% authentic, but it was good in any case.

The stretch to our next stop, Arrow Rock, Kansas, was slow because of the ferocious side wind. We love our Echo, but note that Consumer Reports magazine used the word "tilt-a-whirl" in describing it. The rain began ten miles short of Arrow Rock, and Lena was starting to use the "M" word ("Motel"). The rain stopped, but we could feel a huge storm in the air.

Arriving at the campground, I wanted to set up the tent immediately while Lena registered with the camp host. The problem was that the host talked exactly like Larry the Cable Guy, and he and Lena couldn't understand one another. So I had to translate.

Things turned out fine, and I got the tent up quickly. The awaited rain never came.

This peaceful campground had lush grass and free showers, with only two other campers. After eating our Subway sandwich and reading our books, we fell asleep expecting a symphony of thunder that never came. And the airbed stayed inflated. Yay!

CHAPTER TWENTY-FIVE
KILLER TORNADO

May 13, 2009—Arrow Rock to St. Louis: We didn't have any rain during the night, but we awoke to ominous clouds and scattered thunder. It was still early, and if we left immediately, we'd get to St. Louis way before Jenny woke up. So, we decided to take a quick bike ride. After changing from our "camper" clothes to our "elite cyclist" disguises, we headed off, and it felt great to be riding again.

However, when we stopped to chat with a neighboring RVer, we learned that tornadoes with baseball-sized hail were forecast. Although it would have been good for the journal to get hit by a tornado while on the bicycles (picture Dorothy's mean neighbor floating by the window), we switched strategies from "go for a quick ride" to "get the hell out of Dodge." This turned out to be a good decision, since tornadoes did come through the area later, killing three people.

So we pushed on, and did run into the most intense rain I've ever encountered. At one point we had to pull off the highway and wait it out under an overpass. However, nothing could be as bad as the driving mishap that we once heard reported on our local news.

There is only one TV news station in Eureka, CA. It must be the least desirable station in the country, because we have a steady stream of greenhorn news anchors who apparently can't make it anywhere else. I'm not making this up, we had one anchor with a serious speech impediment, one who didn't speak English understandably, and one who anchored her last broadcast drunk.

The worst one, and the one that was most amusing, was the one who always mispronounced English words. Even everyday words weren't safe, and it was obvious that this woman did not grow up on the planet Earth. We called her the "Storefront Girl," because on one weather forecast, she told us that there were several "storefronts" moving into the area. Did she picture a Gap and a True Value Hardware clomping up Main Street? I shouldn't make fun of her, because there were obviously some defective parts in her brain, but (1) she was hired as a news anchor and (2) it was funny.

The best mispronunciation occurred when she was reporting on a man who had driven his car off the road and into a ravine. It was reported like this: "In Southern California, a middle-aged man drove his car off the road, and spent five days in the bottom of a raven." I can't imagine how unpleasant it would be to spend even one day in a bird's bottom, so with this cautionary tale in mind, we pulled off the road when the storm got too fierce.

We finally arrived at Jenny's apartment a few hours later, and in spite of our near miss with avian rectums, she immediately put us to work packing.

Next, it was over to the hotel, check in, and sneak the bikes into the room.

This was an excellent hotel (Drury Inn)—free beer and wine at night, free long-distance calls, free Wi-Fi, and free breakfast. No leaky airbeds. Can you put a price on luxury like this? Well I can; it came to $165 for two nights.

BTW, our per-night camping fees have ranged from $7.50 to $26, averaging around $15.

After a barbecue at Jenny's friend's house, I lay in the car in a drunken coma while Gunilla guided Lena back to the hotel, and we slept in this thing called "a real bed."

CHAPTER TWENTY-SIX
MEET JENNY

The day of Jenny's birth was the worst of my life. Jenny breathed in some poop (Google "meconium aspiration") during the birth (what a character she was!) and had to be rushed to the neonatal ICU. A nurse told me it could either be OK, or there could be brain damage. Lena wasn't aware of the seriousness of the problem, and I kept her in the dark, suffering through her "Isn't this wonderful and exciting?" attitude. You know how people say "Don't worry until you know for sure that there'll be a problem"? Good luck with that.

But the next day the doctor told us everything was fine, and indeed Jenny has zero deficits, apart from an irrational fear of chickens. Oh, and, she doesn't like artificial banana flavoring. But other than that, she's fine.

Jenny sometimes astonished us. When she made a fuss at night, I was more likely than Lena to tell her that she had to go back to sleep. One night, soon after she started talking, she was screaming in her crib. When I went in there, I heard her say, clear as day, "Oh, no! Not *this* guy." Where the heck did that come from?

When she was one-and-a-half and we were at the San Diego Zoo, I pointed to a tiger and asked Jenny, "What's that?" I'm expecting a response such as "Ti-Ger" or maybe "Giraffe." Her answer, and I swear I'm not making this up: "Sumatran Tiger." Pronounced perfectly. I look at the sign, and sure enough, that's what it was. I know she wasn't an expert in *Panthera* taxonomy, so I assume she had just heard someone else say it.

Another time a young, sedated Jenny was about to have an operation, and the doctor looked in her throat to see what size intubation tube he'd need. Jenny asked him, "What are you, a doctor or a dentist?"

We had reports from others that she sometimes used some verbal expression beyond her years, so I'm guessing she was possessed. Yeah, that's probably it.

Jenny was lucky to inherit the "colorful character" gene from my side of the family, and the "work hard" gene from Lena's. So, she might take a kooky class on "How to Build a Time Machine," but if she did, she would get an A+ in it.

Jenny's melodramatic side was problematic. At age three, she ran screaming from me in the crowded Stockholm airport. There was a real possibility that I'd lose track of her, and my mind's eye still holds the image of her disappearing behind a wall of travelers. Her behavior was so far beyond what people expect, that one woman grabbed me and asked "Är hon din?" ("Is she yours?"). If my Swedish were better, I might have answered, "No, Lady, I'm a kidnapper. Thanks for letting me get that off my chest. Now, can you help me catch her?" I finally caught up with Jenny, and all was well.

So, in spite of the rocky start, Jenny has turned into a great human being. Except for the artificial banana flavor thing.

CHAPTER TWENTY-SEVEN
JENNY ACTUALLY GRADUATES

May 14, and May 15, 2009—Commencement: This was the day to celebrate the event for which we'd been waiting four long years: No more tuition payments—Yay! No, of course I'm talking about graduation day. Yay! There were so many officials that wanted to give long speeches, that commencement was broken up into two days.

We had breakfast at the hotel followed by running on the treadmills. I discovered that running while watching TV and changing channels is not a skill that I've acquired, so there were a few extremely humorous Three Stooges type moments as I windmilled around but didn't quite fall. I'd be a viral YouTube sensation if anyone had decided to video the old guy on the treadmill.

We had great weather. See that nice cap and gown in the picture below? Guess how much one of those costs. The answer: $126,000, after subtracting financial aid. It was worth every penny, though.

Finally, back to the hotel to recover for the second ceremony the next day. This was the ceremony for all graduating students, and there were robes everywhere.

Poor Lena really didn't want this photo in the book, but "Art Governs All" (that's a saying, right?). Anyway, here she is sound asleep during the interminable speeches. Lucky her!

Next, it was on to the famous Ted Drewes frozen custard shop. This was the best frozen dessert I've ever had, followed by the best Indian Food I've ever had, followed by the worst diarrhea I've ever had. Sorry, that's gross, and not true. I made it up because I'd promised it in the introduction. I had to fit the word "diarrhea" in somewhere, and this seemed the best spot. So, "You're welcome," ten-year-old boys who are reading this.

Now that Jenny had truly and officially graduated, we scurried back to the apartment for more packing, and were converted from proud parents to pack mule lackeys. Our mission was to help Jenny move her stuff from St. Louis to Kansas City, where she'd landed a job as an engineer.

CHAPTER TWENTY-EIGHT
PACK IT UP

May 16, 2009—Packing Day: Today was not only packing day, but also Jenny's find-and-buy-huge-bulky-things-while-she-has-the-U-Haul day. In other words, the only time that Jenny could conveniently buy a couch, table, or chairs from Craigslist was when she had a huge vehicle in which to transport them, namely, today. She had all the couches and garage sales selected ahead of time, and early Saturday morning we picked up her U-Haul truck and went shopping.

The first garage sale had a dresser that she wanted, but as we pulled up someone else was carrying it away. The second had a couch and chair. She was on the fence about the couch, but just when she decided it would work, someone else said "I'll take it." We eventually succeeded in throwing an assortment of bulky furniture into the truck.

A set of chairs from someone's garage came with a mud-encrusted, smelly, soccer-ball-sized snapping turtle that had somehow crawled in from outside. If you've ever seen a snapping turtle, you know how someone would give them that name—as in "that guy be snapping my fingers off!"

I tried picking it up by grabbing the sides of the shell, but it had very sharp claws that it raked against my fingers. At least I avoided the snappy end. After we confirmed that the smell was coming from the turtle and not the chairs, we loaded up, and headed off.

In the course of a few hours Jenny had acquired a couch, loveseat, table, chairs and bureau for a total expenditure of $175. I guess we've successfully passed the tightwad gene on to our daughter.

Now to get all this stuff into the truck. U-Haul has nice tidy diagrams showing how the different sized boxes fit on top of one another and they all fit neatly into the truck, like a Rubik's Cube. We had a good laugh over that, because in the real world, things come in all different shapes and sizes, so fitting them in efficiently can be a struggle. At this point, we weren't sure everything would fit.

We finished for the day, and Jenny put together a scrounge meal in an attempt to use up as much remaining food as possible. I tried valiantly to reduce the supply of booze, but had to admit defeat after a while. The Bailey's Irish Cream was the best.

We were exhausted by evening. Since we had packed all the beds, it meant pulling out and inflating our airbed. As soon as I collapsed onto it, I realized that it was partially deflated. That is, it had a new leak! Not again! I couldn't understand what was causing those pinprick leaks. It took me 30 minutes to find the leak and repair it. We had to wait another 30 minutes for the glue to cure, but we finally passed out, ready for the final packing and the drive to Kansas City tomorrow.

CHAPTER TWENTY-NINE
AND MOVE IT OUT

May 17, 2009—Moving Day: Work, work, work, and finally we had an empty apartment and a full truck. It was time to take this show from St. Louis to Kansas City.

We drove off in our caravan—I drove the Echo (with Gunilla) in front, and Lena and Jenny were in the U-Haul behind me. We communicated with our Motorola walkie-talkies and it worked perfectly. It felt like I was towing a trailer with a 500 foot tow rope; I'd change lanes and the U-Haul would change lanes.

At lunchtime, we stopped at JJ's Barbecue for some pulled pork and beef brisket. Here is a picture of the friendly waitress taking our order.

Oops, no, wrong picture. That's a picture of the menu. That's right, you just point to one of the animals on the wall and say "I'll have that."

After another hour of driving, both the drivers were getting sleepy, which called for strawberry shortcake and several cups of coffee. The dessert, split three ways, hit the spot.

We finally arrived at the new apartment. Unloading would have been easier than loading, except that we had one major problem: the couches were too big to make the turn around the landing up the stairs, and were also too wide for the doors to the apartment. After a lot of thinking cap work (picture Betty Boop's "Grampy") we realized that they had to be dismantled somehow. I only had to remove eight bolts to get things apart.

We eventually got everything into her new apartment, and slept soundly through the night.

CHAPTER THIRTY
EVERYTHING BURNED

Like our time in the ICU after Lena's crash, some experiences can only be truly understood if you've gone through them. When someone says "I can't imagine what it's like for you," they are right. I've even found that as time passes, you yourself can no longer really imagine what it was like.

For us, one of those experiences was having almost everything we owned burn in the Oakland Firestorm of 1991. The fire started just one mile from our house, on Saturday, October 19. We had an interesting time watching the helicopters fly right over our house with enormous flexible buckets full of water. Some water would even drip on us as they passed. There wasn't the slightest inkling of *You know, perhaps we should gather photos and backups and such, just in case.*

The fire was totally extinguished on that day, or so they thought. The next day, it flared up again, fanned by violent winds. As that was happening, we were 50 miles away at the Half Moon Bay Pumpkin Festival. We were probably lucky to have been away, since 25 people from our neighborhood died.

According to one neighbor, here's why so many people perished. This is a story that wasn't reported on the news. A house near us looked like a junk yard, with "stuff" all over the place. Remember the joke "You may be a redneck if you cut the grass and you find a car"? That was this place.

When the police came and said, "OK, everyone evacuate, RIGHT NOW!" things were getting dicey. The guy who lived in that house had two cars and he wanted to drive them both to safety, so he asked his girlfriend to drive one while he drove the other. The problem was that both cars had manual transmissions, and his girlfriend didn't know how to drive a stick. At one point, according to my neighbor, the girl stalled the car and no one could get around her. Many of the 25 who died, perished in that mini traffic jam.

Although we were lucky not to be home, we were also unlucky because we couldn't rescue photographs or computer backups. When I told this story, soon after the fire, people would sometimes say, "Hey, you know, sometimes they can rescue information from damaged disks." At that point, I would bring out a jar that held the remains of my 3.5 inch floppy disk backups. In the jar only the metal parts of the floppies are present—the disks themselves had been vaporized. Good luck with the data recovery!

Our carefree life changed the moment we saw the smoke in the hills, while returning from the pumpkin festival. We knew immediately what had happened, turned on the news, and didn't even try to go home. We went straight to Ted and Britta's house, and they put us up for a few days.

The police took us into the fire zone two days later, and we saw, as expected, that our home had been obliterated. The sound board from the piano was nestled in the remains of our second car, three stories below it. You can see the car and piano parts in the right side of the garage in this photo. Together, they were only two feet high.

While we were there, a news crew interviewed me. That's right, I was one of those people saying that obligatory phrase; "I've never seen anything like it." Something interesting about that interview: we had lost everything and I was surveying the pulverized remains of our home, yet part of me was thinking "I'm going to be on TELEVISION!" People are weird, huh?

Fortunately, we had good insurance coverage, and by not trying to squeeze every dollar out of the insurance company, we rebuilt our house in one year. Out of the 3,791 homes destroyed, our house was the 51st one to be rebuilt. Every night all the construction workers in the neighborhood went home, and we were left in this spooky zone of wrecks and half-rebuilt dwellings.

It was sad to lose our home, our photographs, our Hummel figurines (just kidding), but mostly it was just a year-long hassle—rebuilding and dealing with the insurance company. On the other hand, I know that now that I'm detached from the event by 22 years, "I can't imagine what it was like for me."

CHAPTER THIRTY-ONE
AN ECHO ECHO

May 18-21, 2009—Car Shopping: Most of our time in Kansas City was spent car shopping. Jenny did all the brain-work, and Mom and Dad were the chauffeurs—taking her to the different cars she uncovered on Craigslist. It was important to complete this before we left, since she needed us for transportation to the car candidates.

The intergoogle sure helps with buying a used car, from CARFAX reports and user reviews to forums full of enthusiasts devoted to a particular car model. And a GPS is great when you need to drive to ten different owner locations for test drives. In my day, we'd just trudge the five miles through the snow and kick the tires.

This was a major job: Jenny would run a CARFAX report, Gunilla would take us to a car, Jenny would test drive it, and, if interested, take It to an autoshop for evaluation.

We took a break at Warren Buffett's CORT furniture store where Jenny had a gift certificate. While she and Lena were shopping, I amused myself playing with the Warren Buffett cardboard cutout. Here I am giving him some stock advice, which he is not taking seriously. Perhaps he should call Sadie (the dog at my accountant's office).

Speaking of cars, in the midst of all this driving, our Echo reached the milestone of 150,000 miles [as I'm writing this book, it's at 220,000 miles].

Jenny ended up with a 2001 Toyota Echo with only 78,000 miles listed for $4,500. This was just what she'd been looking for. She had the seller meet her at an auto shop where it got a clean bill of health, and after a few hours of haggling, she got it for $4,100.

Note that the above narrative doesn't convey all the complicated logistics of finding mechanics, driving here and there, following each other on the highway, and cell-phone negotiations. These were exhausting days for all.

But we picked up her new car the night before our departure, and packed ours for the trip home.

Turns out there's more to this story. Two years after buying it, Jenny's red Echo had a fender bender. The shop fixing it called her in while it was up on a lift, and said "Take a look at that." An important frame component was dented, and the mechanic said that the car wasn't safe to drive. Apparently the mechanic that inspected it two years prior had missed that.

She easily sold it for $1,400 with full disclosure (people couldn't resist the bargain) and bought a new car. So the moral of the story is that even if you do everything right, and get the car inspected, you still might miss something.

Stay tuned for our first major mishap!

CHAPTER THIRTY-TWO
A MAJOR MISHAP—FINALLY!

May 22, 2009—Kansas City to Sergeant Bluff: Before I get to our major mishap, here's an interesting statistic about the first half of the trip. When I Googlemapped the distance from home to St. Louis, the answer I got was 2,194 miles. That was the straight route. Our actual driving distance to St. Louis was 3,331 miles. OK, perhaps it isn't so interesting, but it shows how much sightseeing we did.

Now to the mishap. I received an automated email alert from our credit card company saying that there was some unusual activity going on. Indeed, it turned out that someone had gotten our credit card number and was testing it to see if it was valid. So, we had to cancel the card and get a new one. Normally this involves a new card being sent out and arriving in a week or so, but that wouldn't work so well on our trip.

According to Wikipedia, 0.1% of all credit card transactions are fraudulent. This number has stayed relatively constant or even decreased over the years due to improved fraud detection systems.

Thieves have many schemes for getting your number, ranging from bluetooth skimmers which, installed on top of a legitimate readers, grab information and send it to a nearby laptop, to waitresses simply writing down the data from the card.

The credit card companies seem to just accept this as a cost of doing business. The cardholder isn't liable for fraudulent charges, but as we found, if it happens at the wrong place and time, it can be a major inconvenience. A real first-world problem.

In the past, I've used Mastercard's ShopSafe program. That is, I generated many virtual numbers, and used a different one for each merchant. This turned out to be more trouble than it was worth, however, since the virtual numbers only lasted for a year, and if your main number was stolen, all of those virtual numbers were also (unnecessarily) invalidated. In any case, since the cardholder is not liable for fraud, the ShopSafe program is useful only to the card issuer.

Perhaps this wasn't a *major* mishap, just a *medium* mishap. However, I've found that without a credit card, one feels like a second-class citizen. You can't reserve a hotel room or campsite, gasoline purchases aren't as quick and easy, and you have to carry more cash. The mishap was putting a crimp in the free-wheeling nature of our trip. So, I wanted to get the new cards ASAP. The problem was discovered on the Friday before Memorial Day weekend, adding to the complication. But with some time spent on the cell phone at a rest area, I arranged for overnight Fedexing (with Saturday delivery) of the new cards. That's why, as I write this, I'm sitting in the lobby of an Econolodge in Sergeant Bluff, Iowa.

Our Econolodge looked a little like a prison, with a rows of doors and windows set into a brick wall. It was indeed our prison until our credit card owner status was restored. But the hotel wasn't bad at all. Small, but clean and comfortable. The rooms smelled slightly of cigarette and fertilizer, but the advantages of being 20 feet from your car outweighed the lack of cushiness.

We once stayed in an awesome Mom and Pop motel in Tonopah, Nevada: The Clown Motel. I asked the owner how to tell, when driving by, whether a motel is good or not. His advice: inspect the outside of the building. If it's neat and well-maintained, you can expect the same for the rooms.

We had planned to go a lot further on this first day of our return trip, but it was better to get the card shipment all set up before late afternoon. We took advantage of our change in plans by saddling up and going on a bike ride in this super-flat region.

We headed out on the straightest, flattest road I've ever seen. There wasn't much change in scenery and no turning or climbing, so it felt more like riding a stationary bike than a real bike. However, the weather was great—it had that nice "thunderstorm coming" vibe.

We've found that roads are not very bike-friendly here in the Midwest, as you can tell from the two inch shoulder in the above photograph. This was true in St. Louis and Kansas City as well. I had gone on a short ride from Jenny's apartment in KC, but had to just tool around the residential neighborhoods, since the bigger roads would have been suicide.

Our Iowa route had a concrete road with no paved shoulder. All but one of the cars gave us plenty of space; they were driving around 60 MPH.

We headed into Bronson, Iowa, a community with perhaps 80 residents, all of whom had credit cards. The ride was 23 miles altogether, and we felt that we had burned off those BBQ calories we'd accumulated.

Did the new credit cards arrive to make us whole again? Find out soon, but first, a word from our sponsor: Pepsi!

CHAPTER THIRTY-THREE
PEPSI COOKING

When camping, there's one stove that's far superior to all the others: The Pepsi-can stove. It's my favorite camping tool, and you can make it yourself by gluing some parts of aluminum cans together and drilling some holes. Here is ours in action:

What I like about it:

- It only costs a few dollars to make (Google "beverage can stove" for directions).

- It weighs less than an ounce!

- It's tiny—you can keep it in your cook kit.

- It's reliable. There are no moving parts (mine has never failed).

- It can burn many different fuels. I prefer "Heet," a gas line water remover, available at all auto parts stores, that comes in a convenient container).

To use it, you simply pour in some fuel, light it, and suspend your pot above it. You can bring a grate with you or find some rocks to support the pot.

CHAPTER THIRTY-FOUR
SECRET DAKOTA CHILD LABOR

May 23, 2009—Sergeant Bluff to Chamberlain, SD: Today was "wait for the credit cards" day, and it started with a reasonably good chain-hotel breakfast (Bagels, toast, and orange juice).

I then camped out in the lobby at 8 AM, working on the journal and waiting for Mr. (or Ms.) FedEx guy. I called BofA to make sure that the cards had gone out, but the answer was ambiguous.

Lena spelled me at 10, and at 10:45 FedEx pulled up with our new cards. There was much rejoicing that involved dancing with the FedEx guy, the lobby clerk, and the woman in room seven. We were made whole again, and ready to resume our trip.

So off we went across South Dakota, flying along at 75 MPH. We made the obligatory stop at the "World's Only" Corn Palace, in Mitchell, SD, which has been redecorated with corn parts annually since 1890.

Mitchell is a small town, with a dark underside. Check out this picture:

You may think this is just a kiddie ride, but it's actually a glimpse into the secret child-labor camps in Mitchell, South Dakota. This train picks up the kids for their 16-hour shifts in the sweatshop. Think I'm wrong? Do you see any smiling faces? Notice the suspicious glances of the driver and the trustie behind him?

We snuck out of Mitchell, and got one of the last campsites at the American Creek campground in Chamberlain, SD. It was a nice place on the edge of the Missouri River. We rode our bikes into town and got food for dinner and breakfast.

Something I've noticed on this trip is that John Lennon was right when he said "Life is what happens while you are making other plans." No matter how much fun we're having, we're almost always thinking about or planning the next activity. When we're driving to the campsite, we're planning what we'll have for dinner. While eating dinner we're thinking about getting the firewood. Around the fire, we're planning the next day. It's like watching a TV program, and having advertisements at the bottom of the screen for the next. If you're not careful, these mini flash forwards will continue until they are cut off by death.

So you have to learn to say, "Excuse me, but I'm watching *this* show now." That is, you have to remember to enjoy what you're doing at the moment. Enjoy the journey. Not always possible, but a worthy goal.

Thunderstorm adventure coming up in the next chapter!

CHAPTER THIRTY-FIVE
AL WORKS A SILVER MINE

May 24, 2009—Chamberlain, SD to Sheridan Lake in the Black Hills: When I gassed up the car for today's drive, I noticed a conspicuous sign saying "Don't leave the gas pump unattended, you will have to pay for any spilled gas." I heard a click after our tank was full, but the gas kept flowing. I couldn't get it to stop. I pulled the nozzle out and pressed the tip against the ground, but it kept flowing. I finally got it to turn off.

When I started the car the pool of gasoline exploded, and flames covered the bikes and the back of the car. No, that was the part I made up. No flames, just a gallon of unleaded on the pavement. I told the gum-smacking girl attendant about the problem, but I had a feeling that they weren't going to fix it. Could they really view that dangerous situation as a profit center?

Anyway, our next obligatory stop was the famous Wall Drug Store. The Hustead's opened it in 1931, but because the town was so small, they just didn't get enough business to survive. Thousands of tourists drove by Wall on their way to Mount Rushmore, but they never stopped. Ted then had the idea of putting up signs on the highway for "Free Ice Water." He did so, and when he got back from erecting the signs, he found a line out the door. The rest is history. Wall Drug was actually pretty amusing, with a fascinating collection of western-themed paintings and other museum-like exhibits.

After scarfing down some pie, we continued on to Badlands National Park. Nice scenery. We were fixing some lunch at the visitor's center, when I noticed an ice machine with some quarters stuck in it. A half-hour's work with my Swiss Army Knife's tweezers, and I was 25 cents richer! It doesn't take much to make a tightwad happy.

Actually, it might have been my inner engineer rather than my inner tightwad that was in control. Engineers can't resist a mechanical puzzle. My favorite engineer joke is this one:

Three people are about to executed by guillotine in medieval Europe, a baker, a cobbler, and an engineer. For the baker, the blade gets stuck halfway down. According to the law of the day, the criminal is free to go if the guillotine fails, and the baker walks away a free man. The cobbler then puts his head on the device, and the same thing happens. He's also free to go. As the engineer is stepping up for his turn, he looks at the guillotine and says, "I think I see the problem."

Engineers can't resist solving puzzles. With the quarter in my pocket, we fixed a simple lunch, and were on our way.

As we came to Rapid City, the clouds were so dark and ominous, that I started wondering whether our 16-year-old, heavily used tent would still do a good job of repelling water. So we stopped at a huge outdoor store, and purchased some tent waterproofing spray.

We had a few showers while scouting out campgrounds, but Lena didn't bring up the "M" word once, and we ended up at the Sheridan Lake campground in the Black Hills of South Dakota. The weather kept the campground from being full, and I put up the tent while Lena set out a rotisserie chicken that we'd picked up at Wal-Mart. I applied the water repellent spray with a cloth (the spray part didn't work), and the rain started just as I was finishing.

Dinner was great, and we only got a little wet; It wasn't as dreary as you might think.

After dinner, we headed in to Keystone to nab some Wi-Fi, and update the journal. Halfway there, the heavens opened up. This was a major-league thunderstorm, and we had to pull off the road twice due to lack of visibility. I didn't have much hope for the tent, which had all our sleeping bags and pillows set up inside. Lightning strikes echoed off the hills every 30 seconds; some were very close.

They didn't have any Wi-Fi in Keystone, so we just hung out, had some soft-serve ice cream, and watched the waterfalls cascading off the roofs.

As we sat there, we considered our options if everything in the tent was soaked when we returned. The first was to leave the tent overnight, and stay in a hotel. We checked a Keystone hotel, but the only rooms they had left were the honeymoon suite and some other expensive suites. The second option was to suffer through a cold wet night. A third was to sleep in the car at the campsite. Fourth, we could pack up all the soggy stuff and head off to a less-populated area and check into a hotel. This all reminded me of a cross-country trip in 1968 with my mother and sister.

We'd had rain much of the way, with the first warm, sunny day coming when we arrived at Grand Teton National Park south of Yellowstone. We hung all the damp sleeping bags and pillows on clotheslines, and drove up to Yellowstone for some close encounters with bears. The deluge came when we were forty miles from camp, and by the time we got back,

105

everything was saturated with water. My mom broke down for the only time during the trip. Although it wasn't in our budget, a night in a motel got things dried out.

Back to Keystone, the rain finally let up a bit, so we got in the car and headed to the campsite. As we drove in, we saw the two young women in the neighboring site packing up their water-saturated tent—not a good sign.

I jumped out of the car, and went over to the tent to rip open the door. Would everything be dry, or would it be a sodden mess? Would we be having a major mishap?

Find out in the next chapter!

CHAPTER THIRTY-SIX
EXPLOSIVE SHOW

May 25, 2009—Sheridan to Devil's Tower: Well, journal fans, time to find out whether we had a major mishap. The tent looked waterlogged when we got back from Keystone. I tore open the door and found that everything was: DRY!

There was much rejoicing, and praise for REI. I had really expected things to be pretty wet. There was a little dampness on one side, but that may have been from a spilled water bottle. Everything was totally dry, not even damp, and we both slept well.

Since this was our first camping stop since the change to mountain daylight time, we were up especially early. Checkout wasn't until 1 PM, so we decided to have breakfast and do some Wi-Fi and sightseeing before packing up. This would allow the tent to dry out a bit.

After a breakfast of pancakes, eggs, and toast, in a Hill City cafe, we did some major journal updating, and then took off for Mount Rushmore and Crazy Horse.

The story goes that a pope was admiring Michelangelo's David, and asked the sculptor how he could create such a masterpiece. Michelangelo replied "Simple. I just removed all the parts that didn't look like David."

The Crazy Horse monument is a work-in-progress, and they are still dynamiting away the parts of the mountain that don't look like Crazy Horse. When we got there, they wanted us to pay $20 for admission, and the thing isn't even finished yet! Gimme a break, right? Instead, we found a good view spot right outside the paid area, and watched the day's scheduled blast. It was OK, but not worth $20.

This whole area (Black Hills) is a bit of a Disneyland tourist place, with reptile gardens, mystery spots, caves, and 5,342 gift shops.

Back at the campsite we put the tent into its official drying-out configuration (that is, upside down), gave it a few hours, and then packed up and pushed on to Devil's Tower National Monument in Wyoming.

We grabbed a secluded campsite with an extraordinary view of the tower.

After slapping a second coat of waterproofing liquid on the tent fly, we hopped on our bikes to ride up to the visitor's center. It was only a few miles away, but a good climb, and a workout because we only had fifteen minutes to closing.

We made it with minutes to spare. Staring up toward the top of the rock, we could just make out some climbers. Although it takes most mountaineers, with equipment, 4-6 hours to scale it, Wyoming native Todd Skinner did it in 18 minutes—alone and with no equipment.

The other interesting story about Devil's Tower is that of George Hopkins, who, in 1941, parachuted onto the top of the monument as part of a $50 bet. He had a rope dropped also, so that he could descend, but it missed, and he was marooned up there for six cold days before being rescued by some mountain climbers.

Back at the campsite, we had a great chicken-apple sausage meal cooked over charcoal. And a great sleep.

Stay tuned for a major change in elevation and temperature. But first, here's a chapter about my wacky inventions.

CHAPTER THIRTY-SEVEN
MORE WACKY INVENTIONS

Actually making or using any of the inventions described in this chapter could result in serious injury, fire, or death. I am describing them here simply for your amusement. Got it?

Most of these inventions are no big deal, but I describe them because when friends see them, they say "Al, what's wrong with you?" But then they'll say, "Huh, that's kind of interesting." And what they mean by "that's interesting," is "Al, there is something wrong with you." I can't take credit for the original ideas, because I usually can't remember whether I thought of them myself or saw them somewhere.

Remote Control Holder: The scientists at Logitech conducted a study to figure out where all the lost remote controls go. Unsurprisingly, 49% were found between the couch cushions, but four percent ended up in the fridge.

The obvious solution is a small board with all your remotes Velcroed to it. Try putting this in your refrigerator absentmindedly. You won't see this on Amazon, perhaps because it's just a piece of wood with some Velcro.

Toothbrush Anti-Germ Structure: If you put your toothbrush in a cup, the saliva/toothbrush conglomeration that's left over from your rinsing will ooze down into the cup and grow little microscopic Jabba the Huts. Instead, this structure will let the toothbrush drain into the sink.

Bubble Wrap Insulation: A lot of heat is lost through our windows, even if we remember to close them. Here's a cheap way to add a little insulation while still letting the light through. This solution is best if you don't actually need to see through the window.

Simply spray the window with water, and press the bubble wrap against it. That's it. Here's what it looks like.

Indoor Motion Sensor Lights: Imagine if you needed to switch on the light in the refrigerator each time you opened the door. Oh, the horror! But seriously, the automatic light in the fridge is a great idea, so why not extend it to rooms in your house? I purchased an exterior motion sensor light and set it up by the door from my house to the garage. Now, if I take basket full of laundry into the garage, the light comes on automatically. And by "if I take" I mean "if my wife takes."

Sliding Firewood Box: Like any self-respecting tightwad, I heat my house for free with wood that I've cut up from downed trees. For many years, I refilled the wood box next to the wood stove by walking armfuls of wood from the door to the box. What a waste of time, and the carpet wasn't happy either. It's better to take the woodbox to the wood instead of the wood to the woodbox. I simply glued some furniture gliders to the bottom of the box, and it slides easily over to the door where I fill it from the wheelbarrow and slide it back.

Fire Blower: Often you need to revive a fire in your woodstove or fireplace or get some embers to flare up when adding some new wood. Most people do this by blowing on the fire, but there's a better way. To understand the concept, imagine using a table straw to concentrate your breath at a discrete part of the embers. This would work fine, but your face is too close to the fire (sometimes sparks are given off), and the straw will melt.

So buy a 2.5 foot section of .5 inch PVC pipe, and glue a piece of smaller diameter metal pipe to the end so that it protrudes a few inches. Finally glue a plastic table straw into the metal pipe, flush with the end. This is what the business end looks like.

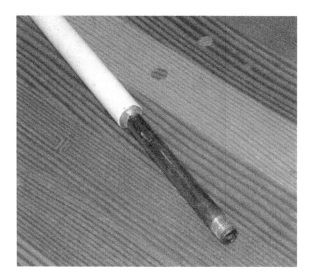

With this blow tube you'll be able to bring the smallest embers back to life. You can turn a sleepy fire into a blast furnace in seconds. Avoid the temptation to use a shorter length of PVC pipe because sometimes you'll generate energetic sparks, and you don't want your face anywhere near those. Plus, you get to feel like a South American blowgun warrior. Just don't inhale.

Bicycle Work-Stand: An adjustable height work-stand makes bike repairs much easier. Fasten 2x4s together as shown in the next picture and attached the result to the wall with a hanger bolt and a wingnut.

CHAPTER THIRTY-EIGHT
AL'S LYCRA CAUSES A STAMPEDE

May 26, 2009—Devil's Tower to Prune Creek: At our campsite, we woke with Devil's Tower framed by the door of our tent.

I had heard what I thought was a wide variety of birds, but when I got out of the tent, I saw that most of these different tunes were coming from a single starling.

I decided to go on a long bike ride, and Lena decided to stay at the campsite. With two long sleeve jerseys and a jacket I was very cold whenever the sun went behind a cloud, but it was an excellent ride, with rolling hills, smooth pavement, and bracing air. Although the speed limit was 65, there was very little traffic, and the shoulder was wide.

A good biking road need only have one of the following: Low speed limit, wide shoulder, or infrequent traffic.

This picture was taken when I was 18 miles from the tower; you can see it on the horizon.

The cows along the route were apparently not used to seeing this weird bicycle/human in lycra thing. One herd ran along the fence with me for a half a mile. Another herd took off in panic and tried to jump a barbwire fence. One calf got stuck, but was free when I came back.

My worst dog experience happened on this ride. It was bad not because of the dog but because of its owner. I was chugging up a long hill, and the dog charged at me out of his yard. I used my preferred technique—I got off the bike, and put the bike between Rover and me. It was a struggle to keep him from getting around the bike, and into my flesh. Sometimes it seemed that he was going to succeed. This was a vicious dog, out for blood. But here's the bad part about this encounter: The whole time, the owner stood on his porch making no attempt to rein in his dog, but simply enjoying the show. The dog eventually lost interest and went away.

I turned around after 25 miles, and got back at lunchtime. Lena had packed up everything. We took off, found a cafe, and I ate a 1/3 pound buffalo burger with homemade fries and a beer.

We arrived at the Bighorn Mountains very abruptly, and headed up over the pass. About halfway across Wyoming, in the Bighorn National Forest, we started looking at campgrounds. We were at 8,000 feet again, and the first campground we came to was closed, and very snowy and wet. The next was Prune Creek. It was also snowy, but open and nice. Apart from the camp host, we were the only ones there.

On the menu was bangers and mash—that is, Aidell's chicken apple sausage and mashed potatoes (from a mix—very good). The wood from the camp host was soaking wet in parts, but after a while we had a nice warm fire.

We went to bed around 9:30 and slept well. On this trip we sleep even better than at home, since we're worn out after each day's packing, driving, sightseeing, and unpacking. The mattress has done great now that we'd learned to pamper it by putting a blanket under it.

Some adventures are coming up: We camp in the crater of an active volcano, and a huge (2,000 pound) mammal comes into our campsite to give Lena the fright of her life. Stay tuned!

CHAPTER THIRTY-NINE
LENA HOLDS BACK A GLACIER

May 27, 2009—Prune Creek to Yellowstone: When we woke it was COLD! I've got a great North Face sleeping bag, but it's only a three-season bag, so I had to use the maximum warmth configuration—totally closed up except for a tiny peephole. This really is an amazing sleeping bag. I've had it since 1992 and it still looks brand new. It packs down to the size of a football.

But as I was saying, it was icy cold, with frost on the grass and car. Lena had the great idea of not screwing around with fires and warm jackets, but just jumping in the car and finding a warm restaurant. Luckily the Arrowhead Lodge was only a few miles away, and was open at 6:30 AM. This was a great place that caters to snowmobilers in the winter.

The 64-year-old waitress here lives in Florida, and every year she chooses a different national park, then gets a waitressing job there for the summer.

The temperature was more livable after breakfast, and we cleaned out the trunk, got things reorganized, and set sail for Yellowstone. Our course took us over the top of the Rockies, and there was plenty of snow at the 9,430-foot pass.

I had expected continuous mountains from here to Yellowstone, but instead there is a wide low plain between the Bighorn Mountains and the Rockies.

The drive into Yellowstone was much further than we had expected, but the scenery was spectacular. Our first wild animal encounter was with a buffalo, followed by a distant grizzly bear. We came upon a herd of cars pulled over to the side of the road, with a crowd looking through binoculars. Most of the people were unaware of what they were looking for, but eventually I got someone to tell me that to the right of that patch of snow, no the other patch, near that ridge by the dark greenery is a grizzly with two cubs. Finally, I could make out three brown dots with the binoculars. Kind of exciting, kind of not. It mostly made me want to get a bear costume and frolic around at great distances while the tourists wet their pants. Then I could move closer and do line dancing. I'll do this next time—I wonder if it's against the law.

My last time through this park (1968), people fed the bears, which resulted in bears walking along the rows of stopped cars, putting their paws on windows and getting handouts. That was dramatic, but the new system is probably better for all concerned.

We got to the campground at 4:30 to discover that it might be full. After much searching, we snagged one of the last sites. The sites are packed pretty closely here, and we were surrounded by other tents and RVs, but we were glad to be able to stop driving. Watching the other campers is always amusing. Our next door neighbor set out dinner for his family. When he turned his back, a raven swooped down and flew off with an entire stick of butter. That is one raven in whose bottom you do not want to be stuck (see the Killer Tornado chapter)!

Actually, this had been a long day, and we were starting to think more about how nice it would be to get home again. Lena apparently has a strong allergic reaction to high-altitude pines, and the Claritin wasn't cutting it. This was my problem as well as hers because Lena's default sneeze is what I call a "scream sneeze." My knee was a bit sore also. Lena, who would be dictator tomorrow (we take turns), announced that we would probably get the hell out of Dodge.

But we had a job to do, so after a great dinner of something or other, probably hot dogs and beans, we went on a hike to the Norris thermal area. Most of Yellowstone is in the crater of an active volcano (last eruption 634,000 years ago, but it *is* an *active* volcano—it says so at the visitor center). About a half mile into the hike, we started encountering more and more fallen trees so there was a lot of climbing, crawling, and detours. Because of the big Yellowstone fire in 1988 the place is swarming with tall dead trees and new trees 6-10 feet high. The dead ones fall all over the place. We finally arrived at the geyser field, and got a good show.

We walked back to the campsite along the road, and fell into bed around 9 PM. There's still a lot of noise in the campground at this hour, but we've got earplugs that filter out all noise, and we slept through until 7:30 AM the next morning.

Wait until you see what 2,000 pound creature greeted us right in the campsite when we woke up. Don't miss it. I know that the "camped in the crater of an active volcano" wasn't quite as exciting as what you expected, but this one will live up to its billing.

CHAPTER FORTY
VISIT FROM A MONSTER

May 28, 2009—Yellowstone Day 2: Here's what we woke up to on our second day in Yellowstone (this is a still from a video you can see at DriveRideRepeat.blogspot.com):

This guy was really big—bigger than he looks here, because the camera always subtracts 400 pounds. He was a few feet from our tent, and Lena did not like it. She just wanted him to leave. Bison are the most unpredictable and dangerous animals in Yellowstone (apart from the nuts that hold the steering wheels).

After that excitement, we had breakfast, and Lena found that with some Benadryl she could keep her sneezing to a minimum. Things were looking much brighter, so we stopped thinking about getting home, and went back to enjoying the trip.

First we went on an 18-mile bike ride then spent the day sightseeing. We had hit a kind of scenic saturation on this trip, having seen so many incredible landscapes, but we could still enjoy the views here. After a lot of overlooks and short trails, paint pots, and geysers, we finally retired back to the campsite.

Good luck and bad luck tomorrow. Stay tuned, but first, a flashback to a real bicycle tour.

CHAPTER FORTY-ONE
THE LAND OF BIG BOWLING BALLS

Bicycle Touring in Sweden: I admit that on this St. Louis trip we wimped out by avoided the rigors of real bike touring (with tons of heavy stuff on the bikes), but we did go on a genuine bike tour once. In Sweden.

There are two reasons to choose Sweden when planning a bicycle tour. The first is this thing called "Allemansrätten."

Allemansrätten is a sounds-too-good-to-be-true law in Sweden. It translates to "Every Man's Right" and says that you can go pretty much anywhere you want in Sweden, and hike, picnic, pick berries or even camp. Nice, huh? As long as you don't actually camp in someone's fenced-in yard, and you don't stay too long, you are good to go. As a result, when you cycle in Sweden there's no struggling to make it the next 30 miles to that campground; you just ride until you want to stop, hop into the woods, and set up your tent.

The second reason to choose Sweden is that in the summer, the days are crazy long. There's plenty of light to be riding your bike even at 10 PM. To illustrate this, here's a story.

On my first trip to Sweden, in 1981, when Lena and I had just gotten married, her friend Bjorn, asked if I wanted to go fishing. I said "Ja," and he told me he'd pick me up later. I was just learning Swedish then and I'd bravely prohibited anyone from speaking English with me. As a result, I found out what it's like to be a dog. That is, my lack of understanding meant that, like a pet, I was always surprised at what was happening next. I'd say something like "Hey, I thought we were going to the zoo today," and everyone would laugh uproariously because I had actually said that I wanted to spread lingonberry jam on Lena's grandmother's buttocks. But when the laughing died down, they would explain that we had changed plans because the zoo was closed. I'd missed that because my comprehension of Swedish was slightly below that of a collie.

I expected Bjorn to show up at around 2 PM, and when he didn't, I figured I must have misunderstood. I waited and waited, and he finally came by at, I'm not making this up, 11:30 PM. We headed out in a river, caught some huge pike, and I got back at 3 AM. I guess the fish there are night owls. The point is that even at midnight, it's still dusk. On a bike tour, you can easily put in some miles after dinner, and stop whenever you feel like it.

Here are a few quick stories from that tour.

This tour happened in 1993. We flew over to Sweden and dropped Jenny off with Lena's parents. I'm proud of our timing here, because as soon as we dropped her off, she developed chickenpox, which lasted only as long as we were on our tour. I'm guessing that a four-year-old with 72 itchy chickenpox marks (yes, she counted them) is an unpleasant thing, so you can appreciate our talent as parents.

One night on the tour, where we stopped to camp, the ground consisted of big, spherical beach-ball-sized boulders. That is, there was no ground between the boulders, it was just huge bowling balls, shoulder to shoulder, as far as you could see. We managed to get the tent to rest on some of these rocks, and wedged our bodies into the cracks between them.

There was another point in the tour when it had been raining off and on for several days. On this day, the rain was pretty steady, and we were struggling along an unending dirt road. Although it was 20 years ago, I still have a clear memory of huddling under a tree (a leaky tree) while waiting out a vicious squall. We were totally dispirited. But just minutes after that, a small but upscale resort magically appeared in this desolate forest. It was the kind of place to which movie stars go to escape. Lena put her foot down, and we checked in and took full advantage of the buffet, down beds, and general pampering.

The third story comes from a night we were camping in a deserted forest. I told Lena that there must be a house nearby, because I heard someone's cuckoo clock, and it wasn't keeping very good time. "No, Einstein," she said "That's an actual cuckoo." So, there's this real bird (called a cuckoo) that makes a cuckoo clock sound—think of that!

We bailed out of our tour one day ahead of schedule, after some all-day uphills, putting our butts and bikes onto a train. For the tour itself, we ended up cycling from Sigtuna to Sveg at a rate of 50 miles per day. We were happy with that. Maybe we're wimps now, but back then, we were somewhat less wimpy.

CHAPTER FORTY-TWO
OLD SOMEWHAT FAITHFUL

May 29, 2009—Yellowstone to East Table: Sadly, even in Yellowstone, Campground Hosts get divorced.

On our way south, out of Yellowstone, we stopped at its biggest attraction. That's right, the gift shop. Ha ha, no, Old Faithful, of course.

To "Agorophobic Al," it was pretty crowded here, and this is the low season. The parking lot here is so large, that it can be seen from space. It's so large that Justin Beiber and Lindsay Lohan could park here and not hit each other. This must be a zoo in the summer.

By the way, isn't it time to stop saying that things are so large that they can be seen from space? Whenever there's a fire in California, Brian

Williams shows us an image and says that it's so big that the smoke plume can be seen from space. I mean, biggus dealus. I can look at a Googlemap satellite view of my house, and see that I need to clean some bird poop off my car. So let's agree that pretty much everything is big enough to be seen from outer space.

Old Faithful wasn't that faithful for us: about 30 minutes late for its scheduled eruption. In the forties, one of the employees found an old truck steering wheel with the shaft attached. He'd stick the shaft in the ground, and his buddy, when he felt the geyser's first rumbles, would yell, "OK, Bob, let 'er rip." Bob would crank the wheel as if opening a big valve, just as the geyser lit off. Each time a few tourists were fooled, and complained about the fake show.

We got a rain check for a free second viewing (just kidding, they are all free), but it was time to push on. By the way, we saw a smaller geyser in Lakeview, Oregon that we liked a lot better.

The lodge at Old Faithful has an old-time rustic charm. Many of the lodges and concessions in national parks have apparently been outsourced to a company call Xanterra. We saw this here and at Crater Lake. The lodges look great, but there's something overly commercialized about them. More "Trump-Tower" than "National Park."

Plenty of great views on the way out, and along the Grand Tetons, but the fire damage from Yellowstone's 1988 fire (which burned 38% of the park) is still prominent.

Since it was a Friday night, we were worried about finding a campsite, so after a good lunch in Jackson, WY, we stopped early in the afternoon at the East Table campground in the Targhee National Forest. It was on the Snake River, and very close to Idaho. It was totally deserted when we got there.

The river was high, and large tree trunks would occasional flow down, making raucous wood-splitting noises when they hit things. We also saw rafters and plenty of pelicans and geese.

The clouds looked menacing, so I prepared the tent for storms that never came.

Great dinner, slept well, blah blah blah.

Stay tuned for thunderstorms and normal people sleeping in filthy bathrooms.

CHAPTER FORTY-THREE
LOW GRAVITY

May 30, 2009—East Table to Bully Creek: After breakfast, I used warm water for washing my hair (mixed some boiling water in with the cold water). This worked great until Lena forgot to mix in the cold water at rinse time—ow!

Next was a quick detour to Craters of the Moon National Monument. This would have been boring, but the whole place is set to 1/6 of normal gravity, making it hard to walk. This is one place where overweight tourists have an advantage.

We drove all the way through Idaho, and got the very last campsite at Bully Creek Reservoir in Oregon. You may have noticed that all the campgrounds on this trip have either been deserted, or almost full.

This place was very well maintained and neat, except for the bathrooms. These, in contrast, were straight out of a third world country with peeling paint and slimy floor surfaces. They also smelled of rotting fish, because the fish cleaning stations adjoined the bathrooms.

Here's a picture of the shower. This picture will be relevant for the next chapter, so keep it in mind.

Am I the only one who sees an image or Geraldo Rivera in the bottom of the shower?

I got in a pleasant ride followed by a nice sunset. Since it was Saturday, and this was a party-type campground, there was lots of drinking and celebrating going on. Our earplugs blocked all that out, and we slept well.

Stay tuned to find out who slept in the bathroom and why.

CHAPTER FORTY-FOUR
GOOD LUCK IS BAD LUCK

May 31, 2009—Bully Creek to Collier Memorial State Park: OK, so you remember the grungy bathroom/shower from the last chapter?

When I awoke around 5 AM and went to the bathroom, I discovered a guy sleeping on the peeling-paint bench right by the shower. I know what you're thinking: "Aw, poor homeless man is so desperate that he's sleeping in the foul bathroom." No, this was a normal, clean-cut 20-something in a bathing suit and T-shirt. He woke up when I walked in, and I asked him "Was it too cold in your tent?"

"No," he said, "I couldn't find my campsite!" He got up stretched, and walked off, saying, "Boy, that's a bad night when you go camping, and can't find your campsite." Think alcohol was involved?

The sun was just coming up, and I got the pancakes going by the time Lena got out of the tent.

Today was strength-training day, which included barbell squats using Lena's 300-pound duffel while the tent dried out. Then we packed up and headed off.

We had thought we'd had great luck in finding a campground soon after dinner even though none showed on the map. But it turned out it was bad luck, because if we hadn't seen the Bully Creek Reservoir site, we would have stopped at a dreary, depressing private campground a few miles further on.

So, I know what you're thinking now: *Al. That doesn't make sense. Why would it be bad luck to stay at a nice campground, and good luck to stay at a dreary, depressing campground?*

Well, here's the answer: Because at the dreary campground, there was big lightning strike, right across the road, and we could have had a front-row seat! We stopped here for ice, and the campground owner showed us the tree that had been struck by lightning the night before.

The strike came right down the side of the tree, exploding off the bark and sending it flying hundreds of feet away. That would have been loud. How often does one get to experience something like that? Well, win some, lose some.

Knowing that lightning doesn't strike twice, we pushed on and crossed most of Oregon. The central part of this state is surprisingly scenic, with dramatic canyons and lakes.

We saw a historical marker sign mentioning "The Perpetual Geyser" in Lakeview, so we kept our eyes open.

Although we saw "The Perpetual Geyser" on the map, when we got to Lakeview, there were no signs for it. We found it anyway, this lone geyser in Oregon, just on the side of a small road, with a fence around it to keep people from burning themselves. It was actually better than Old Faithful, because it went off every 90 seconds or so. Best geyser of the trip.

That night we stayed at the world's best-maintained campground, Collier Memorial State Park. For example, the fire ring is vacuumed out after each guest. This despite signs saying "Due to lack of funds, we have cut back on maintenance."

We prepared some dinner-sized breakfast burritos, and ate our dinner bathed in smoke—something we were getting a little tired of.

When some heavy rain started, we retired and slept with great confidence in the waterproof properties of our tent. It was a little sad because this would be the last night of camping on the trip. But just a little.

133

CHAPTER FORTY-FIVE
AL'S BICYCLING TIPS

This is another cyclists-only chapter, relating some things I've learned in my long career as a mediocre cyclist.

BikeForums.net: If you have any questions about biking, head over to Bikeforums.net and you'll find the answer. If you ask for information about your bike, and post a picture of it, you'll get answers like "That it is a Fibonacci Model 2298, built in Isolabella on March 17, 1993 by Sergio Fumagalli. There are 28 3/8" bearings in the bottom bracket, instead of the usual 26."

Paraffin Chain Lube: On that forum and elsewhere you'll see two opposing camps, oil lubers and paraffin lubers. I always used oil, as you can see from my chain tattoo in the "Al Gets a Tattoo" chapter. Oilers say the paraffin lubing is more work, but I wanted to see for myself. I followed instructions on the web, cleaned the old oil off a chain, let it dry out, then put it in a small slow cooker with paraffin wax from the hardware store. I found that the one lubing lasted over 1,000 miles, and I didn't need the frequent cleaning and relubing that I'd done with oil. The chain always looked clean (that's the most important thing, right?). No more chain tattoos on my legs. Even accounting for the initial setup, the paraffin lubing was much less work. Note that if you ride in the rain, you will have to reapply the wax more frequently.

So, the tip here is to keep an open mind about paraffin lubing.

Pump versus Carbon Dioxide Inflater: Cyclists with small pumps can be burdened with slow, tedious work when inflating a tire on the road, but can handle many flats on one ride. Owners of gas inflaters can inflate a tire in a second, but with too many flats they'll be out of luck. I finally found the solution to this problem: carry both. I can fit a Genuine Innovations Ultraflate, and a Lezyne Tech pump in my small seat bag (shown in the photo below). The inflater is used for the first two flats, and the pump for any additional punctures. Another product I recommend is the Quik Stik instead of multiple tire irons.

How Much to Spend on a Bike: Many cyclists will tell you that you need to spend thousands of dollars on a bike. I got my current bike at a garage sale in 2010 for $65:

Admittedly, that was a lucky find, and I was fortunate to know about bikes and how to fix any defects I found. But with some luck and advice from BikeForums.net, you can probably save thousands by buying a used bike that was top of the line when it came out. That could help you retire early, and do more riding.

When my Specialized M2 Pro was made, in 1997, it cost over $2,000 (about $3,000 in 2014 dollars). A quality bike that is ten or more years old can still give you a great deal of pleasure. Many, like the one I bought, spend years unused in a garage.

Remember that one of your goals in cycling is to get exercise. Yes, it's true that it's fun to go faster or further for the same amount of effort, but unless you are racing, I recommend drawing the line at a lower price point.

Clipless Pedals Practice: When I started riding seriously, I used toe clips to keep my feet securely fastened to the pedals. Nowadays, real cyclists use shoes with a cleat on the sole that clips into a special pedal. Because toe clips are no longer necessary, these new pedals with clips are called "clipless" pedals. This is stupid, but to use a stupid expression, "it is what it is." (The only good thing about that expression is that you can't argue with it.)

Anyway, many cyclists, after they first switch to clipless pedals, will, at least once, fall down when coming to a stop. Their feet stay fastened to the pedals, and down they go.. This is referred to joining "Club Tombay" (from the French verb tomber, to fall). It could result in a bruised ego or a broken elbow. This happened to me twice, and then I found a way to make myself fall-proof.

Here it is: Ride to a deserted street, and start and stop over and over. The key, however, is to practice unclipping at every different possible position of the pedals. That is, unclip with your foot at the bottom, unclip with it at the 9 o'clock position, unclip when you are at the top, etc. Do all of this with your left and right feet. Not only will you cement the unclipping idea in your brain, but you will find that you can unclip quickly if you start to fall over.

Staying Warm: On my typical rides, it is freezing when I start out, and warm later on. I don't want to carry any extra ounces of warm clothing on the latter part of the ride, so I make disposable arm warmers out of old socks. When your socks' heels wear through, cut off the toes, and you have arm warmers for your forearms. Put them on at the start of the ride, and when it warms up, you can either dispose of them, stuff them in your jersey pocket, or hide them somewhere, and pick them up next time you're driving through.

Aches and Pains: I used to get aches and pains from riding my bike (and also from playing the piano). These included sore neck, sore back, sore wrists, and sore shoulders. Now (at age 60), I don't. It's weird how much less pain I have now. This may be due to what I call the "morning sickness phenomenon," or the pain may have been reduced by a program of regular stretching.

What is this morning sickness phenomenon I speak of? More than half of pregnant women experience "morning sickness"—nausea and vomiting that can actually happen at any time of the day. This goes beyond the nausea and vomiting caused by watching perky morning news shows on TV. There are dozens of home cures for morning sickness: go on a liquid diet, eat crackers, eat ginger, avoid sudden moves, go for a walk, eat grapefruit, scarf down cottage cheese, munch on cookies, speak in tongues, wear acupressure bands, and many more.

Not one of those cures has been shown to be effective, but talk to women who have been pregnant, and many will swear their remedy works miraculously. Here's why: morning sickness usually ends around the 12th week of pregnancy, and when it stops, it stops on a dime. One day you have it, and the next you don't.

Each woman with the condition is desperately and successively trying all the antidotes her friends have recommended. So, when the roulette wheel of queasiness stops, whatever cure she was trying that day is the miraculous winner. She's right when she says "I ate anchovies and wood glue on a Saltine cracker, and my morning sickness went away like that (snaps fingers)." But she's wrong in assuming that her sticks-to-the-ribs snack had anything to do with it.

What does this have to do with bike-riding pains? Well, repetitive stress pains can also come and go, and as with morning sickness, you may be fooled into thinking your supplement or routine was effective in eliminating the agony. In my case, it could be that my aches and pains just went away by themselves, around the same time I started regular stretching.

Humans very often improperly infer causation from correlation, and most scientific studies are interpreted improperly on the news. For example, studies showing a correlation between diet soda consumption and weight problems are usually reported as "Diet soda doesn't help you lose weight." However, since those studies tell us nothing about causation, the headline could just as well read "People with weight problems tend to drink diet soda." In other words, despite how things are reported in the media, we often can't infer causation from correlation.

Here's a funny story about correlation and causation. One morning my buddies and I were walking up the hill to our classes at Cornell. When we came to a set of steps, all three of us happened to bound up them quickly. Being teenagers, we thought this was absolutely hilarious, and decided that each time we came to some steps we'd rush up them. That is, we'd walk leisurely towards the stairs, but when we reached the bottom, each of us would make a mad dash up them at our absolute top speed.

Cornell's student union is six stories tall, and extends down the hill, such that you enter at a low level, and climb many stairs to get to the main area. So, we got very good at our slapstick routine. The funny part came when a student dropped a packaged sandwich at the top of some steps just as we got to the bottom of them. The timing was perfect, giving the illusion that we really wanted his sandwich, and were rushing to snag it before he could retrieve it. He incorrectly assumed that it was the sandwich that caused us to rush towards it, and he quickly and nervously grabbed it so that we wouldn't get it. The two events were correlated, but neither caused the other.

With that warning about causation in mind, here's what has correlated with the dramatic decrease in my aches and pains: daily stretching.

When some friends convinced me to stretch more, I read up on it, and got some books out of the library. One of the books described exactly what exercises to do each day, how to do them, and how long to hold each stretch. However, when I multiplied the author's prescribed stretches by the amount of time each was to be held, I realized that he was recommending six hours of stretching per day. I don't think he ever did the math.

So here's Al's Rule of Stretching: It's better to have a very short stretching routine, because otherwise, you're not going to keep at it. My daily routine has 21 stretches in it (I'd tell you what they are, but then I'd probably go to jail for giving out medical advice). If I were to hold each of those stretches for the widely recommended 30 seconds, my routine would take over 10 minutes. I just timed myself, and I went through the routine in 2 minutes, 24 seconds. That's about seven seconds per stretch.

Did you hear that? It's all the stretch authorities saying "Ridiculous!" They say "You won't get any benefit from such brief stretches!" Yeah, well I know myself, and if I had to do it 10 minutes a day, I'd certainly quit after a few months. Perhaps 10 minutes doesn't sound like much to you, but add the 4 minutes per day you're supposed to spend brushing your teeth, and, well, you do the math. I know that when it's bedtime, I'm barely awake, and I realize I forgot to stretch, 10 minutes isn't going to happen.

I started stretching seriously in 2011, and this has made more of a difference in how (relatively) young I feel than anything else I've done. Note that I only noticed a difference after a few weeks of daily stretching. I've read studies that show that stretching before exercise doesn't decrease injuries, and I believe that, but I think there's something magical about regular, daily stretching.

I'll mention one stretch simply because of the funny way in which it was invented. Google McKenzie Method Back Stretch, and you can read about a stretch designed to help with lower back pain. It involves lying on your stomach and raising your upper body, bending at the waist.

Apparently a physical therapist named McKenzie had a patient come in with debilitating back pain.

"Go on in," McKenzie said, "and lie on your stomach on the exam table. I'll be right in."

The therapist got distracted, and when he went in 20 minutes later, he was horrified to see that one end of the table had been left tilted up at 45 degrees. The patient was awkwardly bent backwards at the waist. McKenzie was about to apologize, when the patient said "It's a miracle. I feel a lot better—you're a genius!" McKenzie recovered quickly enough to say "Well, that's enough for today, come back tomorrow for another treatment."

So, in summary, stretching may help you reduce the aches and pains that are often associated with long-distance bike riding. And it will definitely cure your morning sickness.

CHAPTER FORTY-SIX
BACK TO THE SNOW

June 1, 2009—Collier Memorial State Park to Sister's House: The overnight rain stopped by morning and we stuffed things into the car for the last time (yay!) while I watched a chipmunk clean up the rain-soaked tortilla crumbs. Then it was back to the snow again, at Crater Lake, the deepest lake in the U.S.

Like the ride in Zion, a ride around Crater lake (a 33-mile loop) should be near the top of every cyclist's bucket list. I did it on a different trip and found there's a lot more up and down riding than you might expect, but the views are worth it.

Snow removal on Rim Drive is a big deal. The average snowfall is 44 feet per year. They start removal around the end of May, and can only clear a quarter of a mile per day. They usually don't finish until July. In 2013, due to the sequester budget cuts (the snow removal monsters eat $125 worth of gas per hour), they pretty much let the snow melt on its own, and the roads weren't clear until July 22.

The lake boasts a Xanterra-managed lodge, very chichi.

We descended from the crater and arrived at my sister's house in the woods near Medford, Oregon, where we slept in one of those "real-bed" contraptions again.

Stay tuned for the final day of driving, and a summary of the trip with a map, total costs, and total weight gained. But first, here's the final "sidebar" (whatever that is) chapter about an adventure that Lena and I had over thirty years ago.

Chapter Forty-Seven
Puking in a Thunderstorm

Here's a mishap that illustrates the saying "You're on an adventure when you wish you were home wishing you were on an adventure."

In 1982, Lena and I were visiting her folks in Sweden, and we went on a ryggsäcksfotvandringtur. To speak Swedish, all you do is take a bunch of English words, screw around with them, and squeeze them together. For example, in the big word in the last sentence, the only real foreign part is "rygg" which refers to one's back. Other than that it's just "Back - sack - foot - wandering - tour," meaning "wandering around on foot with a pack on your back," or "backpacking."

Apparently we have 1,019,729.6 words in English (.6 really?). In Swedish, the total depends on how you count them. Is "ryggsäcksfotvandringtur" one word, or just five words stuck together? Most Swedish dictionaries have around a half-million entries, but if you count words that are Velcroed together, it has many more.

Speaking of Velcro, it was discovered when Georges de Mestral went for a fotvandringstur, and noticed the burrs that stuck to his pants. The word "Velcro" was added to our dictionary in the year nineteen something-or-other. I've learned that the phrase "Velcro forehead" refers to the overly dramatic gesture of tilting your head back and holding the back of your wrist against your forehead ("Oh, woe is me!"). Can you tell that I'm worried that this chapter is too short, and I am desperately looking for stuff to add?

So anyway, where was I? Oh, yeah, Lena and I were on a shortbackpackingtripinthemountainsofsweden. On our route to the more desolate sections, we passed houses that had sod growing on the roof.

142

And when I say sod, I don't mean the neat, well-mowed stuff you buy at the nursery. I mean long messy grass, other small plants, cuckoo birds, and gophers. And these weren't museum displays put up for tourists, people were really living in these things. It's where we get the saying "People who live in sod houses should throw stones, but no stones from the roof, please."

This was a great place to foot wander, but when we were the farthest from the car, Lena got sick (really sick), and both Lena and the heavens opened up at the same time. It gave me a case of Velcro forehead, and my main memory of that trip is of continually taking tiny plastic snack bags of vomit out and dumping them in the streams of water surrounding the tent.

Luckily Lena's Scandinavian constitution won out over the bugs, and the next morning she was all better and ready to drag me home, out of the wilderness. So, we had a generalgoodtimedespitethepukingadventure.

CHAPTER FORTY-EIGHT
HOME SWEET (AND FOGGY) HOME

June 2, 2009—Gold Hill to Home: We had an uneventful final day of driving, and when we encountered the coastal fog we knew we were almost home.

It felt great to pull into our garage after our big circle of driving around the western U.S.

What did we learn from the trip? Wait a second, we were supposed learn things? Nobody told me that. I think it's enough that we made it there and back, didn't leave the oven on, and didn't spend five days stuck in the bottom of a raven. Also, how many couples can be within a few feet of one another 24/7 for over a month and not end up as a crime statistic?

But let's see, what did we learn? Put a blanket under the airbed. Carry a spare credit card. Buy a roof rack for the bikes. Don't chew crunchy apples near national monuments. I guess the short answer is that we didn't learn much, but we had a great time. We've been on a few similar trips since (in Idaho, Oregon, and Utah), and if you're lucky, I won't write any books about them.

One of my reviewers read the first draft of this book, and said, "But Al, where is the romance?" So I called out to Lena, who was in the other room knitting, "Did we have romance on the St. Louis trip?" and she said, "Yes, about ten times." So now you know that (TMI?).

How many miles did we travel? How much weight did we gain? How much money did we spend?

Find out all these things in the next and final chapter.

EPILOGUE

Trip Statistics: Here's the final map of our adventure:

So, you see, we actually followed the original plan pretty closely.

Here are some statistics:

Total Days Gone: 34
Total Miles Driven: 6,630 (Average 195 miles per day)
Home to St. Louis: 3,316 miles
St. Louis to Home: 3,314 miles

Bicycle Miles Ridden: 280 miles

Average Gas Mileage: 36.45 MPG

Here are the costs. Remember that the dollar amounts are in 2009 dollars. Google "Inflation Calculator" to convert these to current day dollars.

Total Trip Cost: $2,083
Four nights in hotels: $255
Twenty nights camping: $308 (Average campsite cost: $15.40)
Eating at Restaurants: $399
Groceries: $200 (After subtracting a normal month's grocery expenditure)
Gasoline: $398
Other Expenses: $523

Total Weight Gain Lena: -2 pounds
Total Weight Gain Al: -4 pounds

That's right, we both lost a small amount of weight. Possible reasons: (1) Even with the driving, camping life is less sedentary than normal life. There's a lot of walking around, setting up camp, packing, getting water, getting firewood, etc. (2) We lost muscle, since we did less vigorous exercise than on our normal home schedule, (3) I'm lying and we actually gained 40 pounds. Each.

Would You Do Me a Favor?

Thank you for reading my book (or at least skipping to this page). I hope you enjoyed it.

I have a small favor to ask. Could you take a minute and write a short review of this book on the site from which you bought it? I read all my reviews, and enjoy getting feedback about my writing.

Feel free, as well, to send me an email at FoggyBeach@gmail.com. I will personally respond to all the emails I receive, unless I become as popular as Stephen King or J.K. Rowling, in which case someone from my staff will reply to you.

For any updates, or to find out about my other books, please visit AlMacyStuff.com.

ABOUT THE AUTHOR

Al Macy lives in Northern California, the real Northern California (that is, not San Francisco, which is only slightly above the middle of the state, and should be called, at most, upper-middle California), with his wife, Lena. He takes naps, plays jazz piano, goes on bike rides, and writes books. In that order.

Made in the USA
Coppell, TX
21 May 2020

26136253R00085